CHARACTERS OF JOYCE

DAVID G. WRIGHT

CHARACTERS
OF
JOYCE

GILL AND MACMILLAN

BARNES & NOBLE BOOKS
Totowa, New Jersey

First published 1983 by
Gill and Macmillan Ltd
Goldenbridge
Dublin 8
with associated companies in
London, New York, Delhi, Hong Kong,
Johannesburg, Lagos, Melbourne,
Singapore, Tokyo.

7171 1155 5

Published in the USA 1983 by

Barnes & Noble Books
81 Adams Drive
Totowa, New Jersey, 07512

ISBN 0-389-20424-2

Library of Congress Cataloging in Publication Data

Wright, David.
    Characters of Joyce.

    Bibliography: p. 125
    Includes index.
    1. Joyce, James, 1882-1941 — Characters.   2. Joyce, James, 1882-1941 —
Technique.   I. Title.
PR6019.09Z9576 1983   823'.912   83-11919
ISBN 0-389-20424-2

Origination by Galaxy Reproductions Ltd, Dublin
Printed and bound in Great Britain by
Biddles Ltd., Guildford and King's Lynn

To Elizabeth

Contents

Preface

This book grew from my wish to express a series of related perceptions about Joyce's characters. I have written with new Joyce readers in mind, assuming only moderate knowledge of his life and works, especially in the case of *Finnegans Wake*. I hope that some of what I say will interest professional Joyceans as well.

I owe most to Joyce himself, for providing fascinating and inexhaustible texts. I also owe much to people with whom I have discussed Joyce, especially Professor Michael Sidnell, who supervised the University of Toronto dissertation where I first wrote about Joyce's work, Dr Brian Boyd and Professor Don Smith. Dr Terry Locke gave me a useful idea with the observation that Robert Hand in *Exiles* resembles a fusion of Freddy Malins and Michael Furey in 'The Dead'. The students of the graduate class on Joyce which I taught at the University of Auckland helped with their enthusiasm for Joyce and fresh ideas about his writing.

Because most of this book had to be written in New Zealand, out of reach of Joyce manuscript collections, I have made extensive use of the *James Joyce Archive*. My perception of Joyce has been assisted by several of his critics and interpreters; the most important debts of this kind are acknowledged in the notes and bibliography. My approach to Joyce, unfashionably, requires biographical knowledge and I have therefore drawn often on Richard Ellmann's *James Joyce*.

I wish to thank Professor John H. Sutherland, Editor of *Colby Library Quarterly*, for permission to draw on an article about *Finnegans Wake* which first appeared in that journal. I am also grateful to the copyright holders of the texts from which I have quoted, especially to Random House Inc. and The Bodley Head for extracts from *Ulysses* (© 1914, 1918 by Margaret Caroline Anderson and renewed 1942, 1946 by Nora Joseph Joyce), to Viking Penguin Inc., Jonathan Cape Ltd. and The Society of Authors as the literary representative of the Estate of James Joyce for extracts from *A Portrait of the Artist as a Young Man* (© 1916 by B. W. Huebsch Inc., 1944 by Nora Joyce, 1964 by the Estate of James Joyce) and to Viking Penguin Inc., Faber and Faber Ltd. and the Society of Authors for extracts from *The Critical Writings of James Joyce* (© 1959 by Harriet Weaver and F. Lionel Monro).

I am grateful to the English Department of the University of Toronto for making me welcome while I completed this book.

My gratitude to my wife for support and encouragement is acknowledged in the dedication.

D. G. W.
Toronto
May 1983

List of Abbreviations

CW.   Joyce, James. *The Critical Writings of James Joyce*, ed. Ellsworth Mason and Richard Ellmann. New York: Viking Press, 1959.

D.   Joyce, James. *Dubliners: Text, Criticism, and Notes*, ed. Robert Scholes and A. Walton Litz. New York: Viking Press, 1969.

E.   Joyce, James. *Exiles*. Harmondsworth: Penguin Books, 1973.

FW.   Joyce, James. *Finnegans Wake*. Rev. ed. New York: Viking Press, 1958.

JJ.   Ellmann, Richard. *James Joyce*. Rev. ed. New York: Oxford Univ. Press, 1982.

JJQ.   *James Joyce Quarterly.*

L I, II, III.   Joyce, James. *Letters of James Joyce*. Vol. I, ed. Stuart Gilbert. New York: Viking Penguin Inc., 1957; reissued with corrections 1965. Vols. II and III, ed. Richard Ellmann. New York: Viking Press, 1966.

MBK.   Joyce, Stanislaus. *My Brother's Keeper: James Joyce's Early Years*, ed. Richard Ellmann. Rev. ed. New York: Viking Press 1969.

P.   Joyce, James. *A Portrait of the Artist as a Young Man: Text, Criticism, and Notes*, ed. Chester G. Anderson. New York: Viking Press, 1968.

SH.   Joyce, James. *Stephen Hero*, ed. Theodore Spencer. Rev. John J. Slocum and Herbert Cahoon. New York: New Directions, 1963.

SL.   Joyce, James. *Selected Letters of James Joyce*, ed. Richard Ellmann. New York: Viking Press, 1975.

U.   Joyce, James. *Ulysses*. New York: Random House, 1961.

Note: Corrections to Joyce's texts which have been established by scholarship have been adopted in quotations, particularly in the cases of *Exiles* and *Ulysses*. The Penguin edition of *Exiles* has been used because there exists a list of textual corrections based on this edition (see John MacNicholas, *James Joyce's Exiles: A Textual Companion*, 77–108).

Full bibliographical details for other books cited appear in the bibliography. To avoid clutter and duplication, these details are omitted in the text and notes.

A hesitating soul taking arms against a
sea of troubles, torn by conflicting
doubts, as one sees in real life.

Ulysses

1

Introduction

Characters in fiction walk off the page to meet us. They are among the most immediate, engaging and amiable aspects of the novel and the pleasure of encountering them resembles that of meeting new people in what we call real life. All readers respond to fictional characters and may come to regard them as friends, or as reprobates in need of correction. Literary critics, who may wish they could describe works of literature in more austere or systematic terms, are also forced on occasion to acknowledge the 'human interest' of the characters about whom they read.

Investigation of character is particularly applicable to prose fiction. Every novel, after all, contains characters and so our reasonable expectation that we will meet them is never threatened — as the expectation of a plot may be, especially in some recent novels. Even Samuel Beckett, who can envisage plays without actors, sees the need for characters in fiction. A novel with a single character is feasible (*Robinson Crusoe*, a book which helped to establish the novel form, could have been one) but it would still be possible to talk about characterisation. In practice, however, characters living in novels tend to be gregarious.

Characters seem to have become particularly important in modern texts. Earlier novels might revolve around a central figure like Tom Jones or David Copperfield but such characters were usually attached to a solid structure of events. Their relationship to environment, if sometimes difficult, could at least be defined. Jane Austen's Emma Woodhouse requires a plot in which she will be tempted to scheme and which will ensure that she is punished when her schemes go wrong (as they always do). She requires a social context which guarantees her the power to manipulate other people. She thus depends directly on her plot and setting, however lively or unusual her personality. The novel ends and must end when her schemes suffer final collapse, she learns her most important lesson and she moves to a social position where she will have better things to do than scheming.

In many modern novels this kind of appropriate plot and setting fails to appear and emphasis falls instead on characters as unique individuals largely unqualified by events or environments. Modern egalitarianism may have fostered a concentration on the experience of previously neglected character-types, including those who do not fit into society. The apparent arbitrariness of modern history accords with a scepticism about plot, a conviction that ordered chains of events deny our experience of a chaotic and unpredictable world. Novels come to reflect a prevailing doubt that any action is worth taking and so characters may appear trapped not primarily by environment (as in, say, *The Mill on the Floss*) but by their own personalities (as in Beckett's novels). Adaline Glasheen points out that the 'male will' is the most elusive element in *Ulysses*; the same remark could be made about many other recent novels and about the female will as well as the male.[1] New attitudes to environment have arisen in a less stable society in which many people, including some imaginative writers, are exiles.

Characters may now make their way through virtually plotless works where their relationship with setting is shifting and uncertain. It therefore no longer seems appropriate to insist — as critics from Aristotle onwards have — that fictional characters are purely a function of the actions they initiate or suffer. Rather, 'as we move into the twentieth century character often becomes a repository of a vast amount of knowledge and feeling that has a life of its tormented own apart from any serious action in which the author might engage it'.[2] Characters may become a novel's main or even sole reason for existence, so that 'the contemplation of character is the predominate pleasure in modern art narrative'.[3]

A sign of the modern novel's concentration on character and partial emancipation from event and setting is the prevalence of 'stream-of-consciousness' narratives. Extensive use of this mode is largely confined to the twentieth-century novel, partly because the technique took time to evolve but perhaps also because it places greater emphasis on individual characters' consciousnesses than earlier novelists had any reason to require. Stream-of-consciousness narration usually permits us to know a character more intimately than earlier modes of presentation and from within as well as from outside. This new orientation, in which our apprehension of a stream-of-consciousness character fuses exterior and interior observation, the kind of knowledge we usually have of other people and the kind we have of ourselves, can make characters seem remarkably immediate (though whether it necessarily makes them more realistic is a matter of opinion). In any case 'life allows only intrinsic knowledge of self, contextual knowledge of others; fiction allows both intrinsic and contextual knowledge of others'.[4]

Such familiarity and intimacy lead us to take the creation of fictional characters for granted. Yet this process of cooperation between writer and reader is remarkable. An author translates a character into linear narrative (a process which must itself in turn affect the shape of the character) and a reader then reconstructs the character from the narrative. This reconstruction, from printed words to a life-like person approximately resembling the one the author designed, is a significant imaginative act, however common-place it may appear. It is particularly remarkable since the information we are given may be quite limited. There are always gaps in the evidence and all fictional characters are therefore partly implicit. Even in *Ulysses* there are many facts we never find out about the most central character, though it is an index of the peculiarly detailed texture of this novel that we should expect to be told everything about him and find it odd, for instance, that we do not know when his birthday is.

Characters are not present in a narrative until they are mentioned (whereas elements of setting may be implicitly present as soon as we know where we are) but once mentioned they can be assumed to possess two eyes, two legs, etc., unless otherwise specified.[5] (Our assumption of this anatomical normality does not necessarily lead us to 'see' the characters. Characterisation may be a much less visual process than we assume or imply when we talk of 'portraits' of people in fiction. A character's hair colour may be unspecified, for example, but this omission will not prevent us from imagining the character.) But what is the extent of our characters' self-knowledge? Or their taste in politics — or food? And just where does such speculation encroach on supposedly forbidden territory, such as that which we enter when we ask how many children had Lady Macbeth? What distinguishes those characters about whom it is profitable to speculate from those about whom we seem to be told nearly everything we are supposed to know?

Because of such uncertainties, it is possible that the character we reconstruct from a novel may differ in some respects from the one the author put in, and also from the one another reader takes out. Authors must often be amused to see characters intended to be despicable winning a few readers to their own side: Van Veen in Vladimir Nabokov's *Ada*, for example. Critics may disagree among themselves about a character; some, like Richard 'M. Kain, have seen Leopold Bloom as a 'pathetic little man', while others (clearly the majority at present, though fashions may change again) see him almost as a model of humane virtue. Molly Bloom has seemed to various readers to be anything from an earth-goddess to a prostitute and debates have raged on this issue just as if she were a real woman who could be proved conclusively to be one or the other. In such cases, readers may have to accept that a fictional character is 'ambivalent' or 'contradictory'. Yet they can usually attain a remarkable standard of agreement about the nature of a character. How does this agreement occur when the presentation of the character may be oblique, cryptic or otherwise problematic?

Despite the central position and prominence of character in the novel the subject has not been deeply analysed by recent critics. There are numerous studies of particular characters but few of the process of characterisation itself. It may be that the process has not seemed problematic, perhaps because fictional characters can often be satisfactorily discussed in terms we would use to describe real people, terms of which we have a vast supply. Enterprising (and presumably leisured) researchers have extracted from *Webster's Dictionary* nearly eighteen thousand descriptive terms for character-traits.[6] The ability to discuss something with ease creates an impression of understanding which may be deceptive and in the present case this facility may help to explain why more probing analyses of characterisation have seldom been made.

As recently as 1927 E. M. Forster in *Aspects of the Novel* proclaimed a distinction between 'flat' and 'round' characters, terms which seem to imply a direct relationship to the three-dimensional reality of living people. But he says little about the ways in which novel characters come to assume these shapes. Moreover, 'any amount of critical work on the novel in the '30s and '40s . . . begins by aggressively denying any interest in character. Thus the fashion, by mid-century, had shifted so completely that it had become virtually impossible, in serious critical circles, to say anything at all about character as such.'[7] New Criticism seems mostly uninterested in fictional characters, perhaps because, unlike plots, characters are seldom created through the concentrated and intricate textual strategies which New Criticism investigates with greatest zest. New Criticism thrives on specific detail, while characters may be conveyed by diffuse means, so that their personalities accumulate insidiously during a novel. Structuralist critics, too, appear to interest themselves in characterisation only when the characters are attached to and illustrate aspects of a plot. The few attempts which have been made by recent critics to classify character-types systematically have not been especially helpful.[8] It may also be true that 'there is built into *any* critical theory – simply *because* it is a theory – a dislike of muddle and loose ends'.[9] Character and characterisation may tend towards muddle and loose ends and so antagonise the theorist who consequently directs critical attention elsewhere.

Even though (or precisely because) we take the process of characterisation so much for granted, it seems worth investigating further. This study concentrates on different methods of characterisation in terms of the areas of reality on which they draw. It considers what happens when characters are based on real people known to the author and studies in particular characters based on the author himself, whom we can loosely call autobiographical characters. What are the implications for interpretation of basing a character on an authentic source in this way, especially in cases where the author knows that readers will be aware of what is going on?

A novelist (or short story writer or even dramatist) may base his characters on various sources. At one theoretical extreme there is the character created from sheer imagination with no trait modelled on a particular living person. In practice it seems improbable that such characters should exist in a pure state; like certain unstable chemicals, they appear only in compounds. But we can talk about characters based primarily on imagination rather than on living sources. A second type of character is conspicuously or confessedly modelled on a 'real' prototype or on a conflation of prototypes. And a third type is based on the author's own being or on a combination of the author and one or more others. A character created to contrast with the author might seem to be a fourth type but is really a variant of the third, since the author's own attributes are still the basis for the character's shape. There may be other sub-groups of characters — such as those based primarily on literary models rather than living people — but they will not concern us so directly here.

Distinguishing among these types, except in a vague fashion, requires some knowledge of the author's circumstances. The application of such knowledge is unfashionable in current criticism, where for many critics the ideal is still to treat the work, as far as possible, as a thing in itself, or in relation to other texts or to reader responses — but not in relation to the author's life or intention. There is no doubt that these emphases have prevented many critical abuses, thus serving their original purpose but such methods can be applied too puritanically. Authors are free, if they wish, to try to convey meaning through the ways in which they base characters on real people or on themselves.

A critical school may argue that such methods are not a legitimate area of inquiry but this argument will not prevent authors from adopting them. It would be almost as misleading to deny the imaginative presence of real persons (James Joyce, Oliver Gogarty and others) in *Ulysses* as to deny the imaginative presence in the same novel of a real place, Dublin. Such methods of communication, in terms of character, have not been studied extensively. Yet an author's relationship to the sources of his characters can reveal much about his outlook and his sense of the purposes of his writing.

This book studies aspects of characterisation in the works of James Joyce. It does not claim that what applies to him necessarily applies to other writers. Characterisation, as we have already seen, is an aspect of fiction which seems especially resistant to systematic classification. At the present stage of criticism, it is difficult to imagine a paradigm which could usefully relate the characters of Joyce to those of Dickens and Jane Austen (or even to those of Virginia Woolf and Forster). Nevertheless, any study of a single author, if it is based on vital aspects of his work, will suggest ways of examining those aspects in the work of other writers.

Joyce has very few characters created, even partially, from sheer imagination. Bloom is his most imaginatively conceived character but Bloom is also the most complex and derivative in origin, incorporating elements of our two other categories as well. (This is not to overlook the kind of imaginative process required to make use of those models, of course.) Beatrice Justice, in *Exiles*, does seem to have been created largely from imagination and while her chilly nature appears to be intended and to have meaning in the play, she does not become a particularly convincing character: Joyce seems most successful as a 'creator' of character when he has a specific model in mind.

Joyce has numerous characters based in part on other people. Bloom figures again here, borrowing traits from Joyce's friend Italo Svevo, among others. There are many purer examples, such as the priest in 'The Sisters', Davin in *A Portrait of the Artist as a Young Man*, Father Conmee in the *Portrait* and in *Ulysses*.

Finally, there are the characters based primarily on Joyce himself. Stephen Dedalus is the most conspicuous and purest example, though even he acquires a few traits from Joyce's brother Stanislaus. Bloom derives some characteristics from Joyce as well; so do Gabriel Conroy in 'The Dead', Richard Rowan in *Exiles* and others.

Joyce said that he lacked imagination, that he could not create material. This judgment is harsh — the 'Ithaca' episode of *Ulysses*, for example, shows a remarkable imagination — but Joyce was really calling attention to his extraordinary ability to take existing material and rearrange it for his own purposes. His early works transcribe the world with remarkable directness: his epiphanies and *Stephen Hero*, which was partly assembled from epiphanies, rearrange existing facts without significantly changing them (though of course the mere selection of particular facts for use gives an artistic shape to the transcription).

In *Stephen Hero* we also see Joyce trying to solve the problem of finding a suitable voice, something he had not achieved in his early essay 'A Portrait of the Artist'. It may be that this search for a suitable voice led him to investigate more closely the way in which character determines voice and hence to enquire into the varied possibilities of character itself. Thus his next distinct phase, begun soon after he started work on *Stephen Hero*, involved various characters modelled chiefly on other people — the basis of the *Dubliners* stories, most of which can be seen as studies of particular characters or types. In *Dubliners*, still, we sense the cool transcription of an existing world rather than the construction of a new one.

In the *Portrait* Joyce studies the development of a character, a process which here determines the shape of the entire novel. It has been heroically argued that the character should not be associated with the author, Nabokov remarking that 'critics tend to identify Stephen with young Joyce himself, but that is neither here nor there'.[10] Denying this association has the advantage that it allows us to see Stephen as the autonomous narrator of his own story and thus to sidestep the problems of irony and authorial distance which have dominated criticism of the *Portrait*, sometimes unproductively. Yet ignoring this relationship denies what we see — as if we were to pretend, for purposes of analysis, that a brightly coloured butterfly was really black and white. Our fascination with the relationship of Joyce and Stephen is real and something the novel seems designed to elicit. Joyce uses the *Portrait* to explore not only the development of a particular artist (Stephen Dedalus) but also the relationship of another artist (himself) to the material (a character, Stephen) he uses in his work.

Another stage was necessary on the road to *Ulysses* and the appearance of Joyce's most satisfying characters: the writing of his single play, *Exiles*. Characterisation in plays differs from characterisation in novels, with which we have been chiefly concerned. Characters in plays, for example, are less 'implicit' than characters in prose fiction. The playwright exercises more direct (though normally less complete) control over his audience's imagination than the novelist or short story writer does, though he usually must share the details of that control with producers and actors. For example, visible parts of a character's body not mentioned in the text become present explicitly rather than implicitly on the stage and his hair unless lost or deliberately concealed must be a particular colour, which it need not be in fiction. Nevertheless, in the case of *Exiles* we find a 'novelistic' quality which undermines the certainty normally attainable in drama. The reality apparently bestowed on the characters by their physical existence on the stage, or by the reassuringly firm presence of their names beside their speeches in the printed text, is deceptive. In any case, since one of Joyce's aims in writing the play was the refinement of his methods of characterisation, it must be considered here.

After *Exiles* Joyce seemed happier about inventing aspects of character, as Bloom illustrates. The richness of *Ulysses* is in important ways the richness of Bloom which in turn rests in important ways on the complexity of his sources. The meeting of Bloom and Stephen is the central event in Joyce's work and its meaning depends in part on the origins of the two characters, as a highly-autobiographical Stephen meets a Bloom who is partly autobiographical but has several other sources as well. The ways in which each of them is standing in for the author colour — even, arguably, determine — our estimation of the significance of the encounter. Joyce's intermittent depiction of Stephen and Bloom as characters of the same kind (when he knows they are not and knows that we will know that they are not), is a deliberate and amusing technique, which we will miss if we are determined to suppress such autobiographical associations.

Finnegans Wake still poses formidable problems for readers, critics and readers of critics. Copious and often skilled annotation has clarified some of the verbal surface without necessarily making the whole work seem more comprehensible. In its characterisation the *Wake* appears to continue a process discernible in *Ulysses* in which 'Joycean' and 'non-Joycean' elements move closer to fusion and identification between author and character (or characteristic) becomes ever stronger.

In considering a particular text by Joyce, it is often possible to avoid the question of character sources. But when we consider the succession of his texts, patterns of authorial presence and absence in the characters become both conspicuous and compelling. Joyce's philosophy is inseparable from the matter of his personal intervention in his various texts and it is particularly significant that this fact becomes conspicuous when the works are compared: to some extent, it is the differences in the author's strategy among the works which establish the kind of meaning we are seeking.

Joyce's largely plotless works throw great emphasis on character. His only work which depends significantly on plot in the usual sense is the *Portrait* and there the plot can be equated precisely with the development of a character. The *Dubliners* stories mostly resolve themselves through moments of revelation, rather than incidents and what is revealed is often the true nature of a particular character, whether that revelation is made only to the reader (as in 'Clay') or to the character as well (as in 'Araby' or 'The Dead'). *Ulysses* emphasises character and setting more than plot and our dominant impression of *Finnegans Wake*, apart from its bizarre linguistic texture, is of its personalities rather than its events.

Character, moreover, seems to become increasingly fluid as we progress chronologically through these works. Joyce begins with characters who seem a function of their environment (as in *Dubliners*) and moves to characters whose environment seems subordinate to them (as in *Finnegans Wake*). This reorientation accords with a movement from external to internal reality which is also visible in other aspects of the texts. From lost and isolated individuals seen from outside, as with most *Dubliners* characters and Stephen's friends in *Stephen Hero*, we move to characters whose minds we inhabit and whose environment is increasingly determined by the way they see it. Ireland, Stephen says, must be important because it belongs to him (*U* 645).

Thus the problem of relating to the surrounding world is usually mediated for Joyce through the relationship of author and character. In his early work there is a split between 'self'-characters and 'other'-characters, imitating an alienation between the self and the world. In *Ulysses* there is a fusion in Bloom who combines Joycean and non-Joycean attributes in perhaps equal proportions. Bloom's appearance in Joyce's work corresponds to the moment of the imagination's fullest acceptance of the outside world as a distinct entity. In *Finnegans Wake*, despite the proximity of author and character, the status of the external world is more problematic.

Joyce's way of addressing us, throughout his works, rests on intimate relationships between author and character and between character and reader. Hugh Kenner has suggested that Joyce bases all his characters on himself in that he creates them by imagining ways in which (given different luck) he might have become or resembled them.[11] Certainly he always seems to have speculated about the connection between a character — any character — and himself. At some level, most fictional characters do presumably bear a personal relationship, however distant, to their author but Joyce is particularly assiduous in the way he investigates such relationships and makes them not only means to an end but ends in themselves. At the same time he expects us to see the affinities between his characters and ourselves. It has been said that Joyce's writing is satisfying not so much because we come to understand it but because, in it, Joyce comes to understand us. Such 'understanding' is mediated through his characters and the responses they evoke in us.

One reason for the lifelike quality of Joyce's characters is his habit of presenting them to us as if we already know them. A familiarity — more logically assumed by Joyce in the case of people who did 'in fact' exist — substantiates and gives assurance to the intimate bond we are expected to feel with created characters. In this way, Joyce's characters contribute richly to a central concern which colours all his work. The reality which the imagination processes, he would claim, becomes immediate and familiar because beneath our differences we all have similar ways of perceiving it.

2

Dubliners

Dubliners seems at first sight to be Joyce's most detached, impersonal work. Closer inspection shows Joyce, self-absorbed as always, becoming even in these cool stories the personal measure of all he depicts. Throughout his writing he connects his characters with himself by contrast as well as by affinity; both strategies allow him to base his characters ultimately on his own contours. In *Dubliners*, almost as much as in the *Portrait*, people and events depend for their nature on Joyce's view of himself and his experiences.

The years in which Joyce wrote *Dubliners* (1904–7) were busy ones for him. As his letters of the time amply demonstrate, his rapidly-changing and often difficult personal circumstances made him brood intently on his own situation and compare his life with other actual or imagined lives. He continued to reflect on recent or new experiences which were tests of personality and material for literature as well: the death of his mother, his estrangement from his family, his relationship with Nora Barnacle, the birth of a son, his status as a writer – a secular priest of the imagination – and his position as a voluntary exile from Ireland, bringing his relationship with Dublin to a state of crisis and partial resolution.

All of these concerns can be traced in *Dubliners*. Thus, while Joyce's brother Stanislaus claimed that only 'An Encounter' and 'A Mother' were based on personal experience,[1] most of the stories are indebted to Joyce's processes of self-evaluation, self-definition and self-justification at the time of writing. (Ironically in view of Stanislaus' remark, 'A Mother' and the other stories of 'public life' now seem further from significant personal experience than the rest of the collection.) These processes are worked out in various complex ways and there are signs that Joyce planned the collection with this autobiographical purpose in mind as well as with the aim of producing an educational tract and mirror for Dublin's populace (the purpose he suggested in letters to potential publishers). Changes made to 'The Sisters', written before Joyce's departure from Ireland and revised after it, have this private purpose as well as the more public one; 'The Dead' was also added from partly autobiographical motives. As Joyce came to envisage the collection in its final form he sought to make more consistent and purposive his personal appearances in the text.

It is commonly held that in *Dubliners* Joyce presents images of himself as he would have become had he stayed in Dublin in order to justify, to himself or to others, his decision to leave. In one sense it is more reasonable to make this assumption about *Dubliners* characters than about Stephen Dedalus: Stephen is always younger than the Joyce writing about him and we are therefore likely to notice differences between him and Joyce as he was at the same age;[2] such *Dubliners* characters as Father Flynn and James Duffy are older and are therefore characters Joyce might still have grown to resemble. Yet a moment's reflection on these characters shows that such relationships should be interpreted with the same irony Joyce applied to depicting them. Joyce probably did not imagine that he would become a Father Flynn, though he may use the image of this priest (another James) to dramatise his conviction that he had been right to turn away from the Church. Where Joyce does depict characters he might have grown to resemble had he remained in Dublin, he treats them not with contempt but with a kind of benign amusement, a blend of sympathy and judgment, cooler than but similar to his manner of treating his 'own' past in *Stephen Hero*, a mood which represents his acceptance of life's possibilities rather than a rejection. This mood is clearest in the presentation of Gabriel Conroy.

The years when Joyce wrote *Dubliners* were also the years when he tried to write *Stephen Hero*. That enterprise confirms Joyce's autobiographical orientation during this time and there are important connections between the two works. If *Stephen Hero* defines Joyce's present position by analysing his past states, most of the *Dubliners* stories define him by a contrast which is closer in time but detached by geographical and emotional distance. In other words, *Stephen Hero* treats of a Joyce-like character defying Dublin at a time when Joyce was in fact living there; *Dubliners* mostly shows characters contrasting with Joyce and defeated by Dublin at a time when he had achieved intellectual detachment from the city or had actually left it. The exception in *Dubliners* is the first triad of stories, which do depict a past Joyce-figure; they may have been worked up from discarded *Stephen Hero* material. In *Stephen Hero* the author is explicitly included in the action; in *Dubliners* he is implicitly excluded. Yet this very exclusion, the fact that most of the characters are contrasted with his own situation, brings that situation into play to provide a basis for the contrasts.

Joyce associates himself with his characters in various ways, often facetiously or ironically. A playful or sardonic exploration of possible author-character affinities colours many of the stories and lightens their tone like a private joke in a serious speech. In such cases the suggestion seems to be that Joycean wit and self-insight could provide a way out of the impasse in which many Dubliners find themselves; so, presumably, can the attention of the reader who notices such things. Joyce also uses these associations to explore, fix, defend or modify his present position in relation to the society about which he writes. Three main images which Joyce uses in this way are those of the traveller, the writer and the priest.

Thus, allusions to overseas travel are usually made with implicit glances at Joyce's own recent voyages. These allusions relate to the 'paralysis' motif of *Dubliners* and also anticipate Joyce's treatment, in *Ulysses*, of a modern Odysseus who never leaves Dublin. Such allusions even extend to the accoutrements of the traveller. References to nautical clothing recall Joyce's fondness for such apparel, particularly for a yachting cap, a token of his 'difference', panache and mobility. Lenehan in 'Two Gallants' has the cap, Joyce's white rubber shoes and a 'jauntily slung waterproof' as well (*D* 50). Corley's girl wears a 'white sailor hat'. These attributes reinforce the affinity between Lenehan, who lives Corley's experience vicariously rather as a writer does that of his characters, and the girl.

Lenehan's marine garb ironically illustrates the fact that he is not sailing anywhere, unlike Joyce who had already been away; Lenehan spends the story wandering around central Dublin in tight circles. A similar irony marks the end of 'After the Race' where, after a broad sweep of exhilarating movement from the west of Dublin to the east – mostly by racing car, in this book of paralysis – Jimmy Doyle and his companions end the story on a yacht anchored in Kingstown Harbour. The anchored yacht's name is the *Belle of Newport*, but it will not carry Jimmy to any 'new port', though he may wish that it could do so as he regrets the money he has lost in the present one and reflects on his inferiority to his Continental companions – named after people Joyce knew in Europe – and his entrapment in Ireland. The yacht is American and the ending of this story balances that of its predecessor 'Eveline', where the protagonist was similarly unable to take a ship to the New World.

In 'A Painful Case', Mrs Sinico's husband is a sea-captain. No doubt Joyce gave him his profession partly to facilitate his wife's relationship with James Duffy, though such strategies are jokes with Joyce. More significantly, the travelling of the husband emphasises the stasis of the wife; Mrs Sinico's earthbound existence ends under the wheels of a train. There are links here with 'Eveline', where another woman is left behind by a seagoing man, though Eveline's choice not to board the ship is her own even while it springs from panic rather than deliberation. Sydney Parade, where Mrs Sinico meets her fate, recalls Melbourne, where the priest in 'Eveline' has gone: in both cases there is a sad contrast between an allusion to a distant place and the fixity of the character in the story. In an early manuscript version of 'A Painful Case', James Duffy reflects that he could not have taken Mrs Sinico abroad either: 'He asked himself what else could he have done – carried [on] a furtive comedy which must have ended in mutual disgust or gone away with her out of Ireland. Either course would have been impossible[,] the one an undignified intrigue[,] the other a ridiculous elopement.'[3]

In 'An Encounter', the boys dream of escape by ship: 'Mahony said it would be right skit to run away to sea on one of those big ships and even I, looking at the high masts, saw, or imagined, the geography which had been scantily dosed to me at school gradually taking substance under my eyes' (*D* 23). This revery anticipates Stephen's vision, at the end of the *Portrait*, of 'the black arms of tall ships that stand against the moon, their tale of distant nations' (*P* 252).[4] In 'An Encounter', however, there is an immediate moment of bathos: 'We crossed the Liffey in the ferryboat, paying our toll to be transported in the company of two labourers and a little Jew with a bag.' The narrator then fails to read the inscription on a Norwegian ship, further demonstrating his lack of preparation for Continental experience.

In each of these cases where voyaging or related matters are invoked it is clear that Joyce has in mind his own recent experiences, even when, as in 'An Encounter', the basic situation treated in the story had in fact happened to him many years before. The fact that Lenehan dresses like Joyce ironically serves to show how different they are in more significant ways. Unlike Lenehan's, Joyce's nautical outfit was not simply an affectation (though it was that as well) but a token of his voyaging, literal and imaginative, to Europe. Their responses to experience do seem superficially similar: Lenehan 'had walked the streets long enough with friends and with girls. He knew what those friends were worth: he knew the girls too. Experience had embittered his heart against the world' (*D* 58). This could be Stephen at the end of the *Portrait* in one of his blacker moods. But while Lenehan soothes himself with a meal, Joyce's more ambitious response was to leave what he disliked behind him and seek a new life, just as he escaped from the mercantile sexuality associated with the Dublin of 'Two Gallants' into the kind of relationship about which Lenehan can only daydream.

Unlike Jimmy Doyle, whose name resembles his as closely as Lenehan's clothing resembles his, Joyce had not merely boarded a ship but actually sailed away. Far from being exploited by the Europeans whose names he bestowed on Jimmy's acquaintances, Joyce had profited from them, at

least by way of moral support; and he had known them on
the Continent, their own territory, whereas their namesakes
in 'After the Race' appear as invaders: 'Through this channel
of poverty and inaction the Continent sped its wealth and
industry' (*D* 42). Unlike Captain Sinico and Frank, Joyce
had made or would make a voyage not alone but with a
woman (Joyce's departure with Nora was still in the future
when 'Eveline' was first written but the possibility was in
his mind). The contrast is also clear between Joyce's
accomplished and serious departure from Ireland and the
'Encounter' boys' dreamy and frivolous plan ('it would be
right skit to run away to sea'). Unlike the narrator of this
story, Joyce had some knowledge of Norwegian, which he
had learnt in order to read Ibsen. His knowledge of other
places — Ibsen's homeland, for example — had not been
'scantily dosed' into him but actively pursued by himself.
Joyce could 'decipher the legend' (*D* 23) — both the language
and its implications — which baffle the boy in the story.

   More directly, Joyce explores ironic affinities between
himself and his characters by making several of them into
writers. Even the belligerent and insensitive Farrington in
'Counterparts' is required, by Joyce as well as by his boss,
to write for a living. Little Chandler, whose name suggests
that he is an impotent provider of small illuminations,
aspires to be a creative writer in an attenuated but recognis-
ably Joycean manner: 'He could not sway the crowd but he
might appeal to a little circle of kindred minds. The English
critics, perhaps, would recognise him as one of the Celtic
school by reason of the melancholy tone of his poems;
besides that, he would put in allusions' (*D* 74). What writing
he does in reality is presumably confined to his work as a
law clerk.

   Ignatius Gallaher is a journalist, but his inability to write
anything on Joycean lines is obvious — and confirmed by his
prurient attitude to Continental society. In 'A Painful Case'
James Duffy, like James Joyce, translates Hauptmann and
like Stanislaus Joyce keeps a kind of diary. He has 'an odd
autobiographical habit which led him to compose in his
mind from time to time a short sentence about himself containing a subject in the third person and a predicate in the

past tense' (*D* 108), also a Joycean habit, manifesting itself at this time in *Stephen Hero*. But Duffy's squeamish fussiness (he 'abhorred anything which betokened physical or mental disorder') and his inability to enter freely into a relationship distinguish him sufficiently from Joyce and demonstrate that he never could be a Joycean creative writer because he lacks the courage to undergo or pursue experiences worth writing about.

Further *Dubliners* characters are bookish. The narrator in 'An Encounter' and the old man he encounters share this interest; so does the narrator of 'Araby'. (In 'An Encounter', the old man's 'ashen-grey' moustache faintly recalls the ashpit where the narrator hid his books.) The two boy narrators and the old man also share an interest in sexuality and there are suggestions that books provide a way to sexual knowledge. The 'Encounter' narrator especially likes books 'which were traversed from time to time by unkempt fierce and beautiful girls' (*D* 20). The old man remarks that 'there were some of Lord Lytton's works which boys couldn't read. . . . Then he asked us which of us had the most sweethearts' (*D* 25). The narrator of 'Araby' lingers over some of the same erotic images the old man had suggested, especially that of girls' 'soft hair' (*D* 30); this connection may subtly hint that the two stories are narrated by the same boy and that in 'Araby' he has found the sweetheart he claimed to lack in 'An Encounter'. Books and sexuality are further associated as the 'Araby' narrator tries to approach Mangan's sister: 'When she came out on the doorstep my heart leaped. I ran to the hall, seized my books and followed her.' In these cases Joyce is playing with the notion that books contain dangerous information and suggesting instead that they offer a liberation, the kind of liberation he was hoping to achieve through *Dubliners* itself: the freedom which comes from confronting truth fearlessly.

References to the priesthood, which are particularly prominent in the first three stories, are hardly unexpected in a work set in Dublin, remembering that Joyce had contemplated this calling. That he had such a personal association in mind in *Dubliners* seems to be confirmed by the close relationship between a priest and the autobiographical narrator in 'The Sisters' and 'Araby'. In 'The Sisters' the priest instructs the boy in the mysteries of the Church; in 'Araby' the boy chooses for himself which aspects of the priest's life to contemplate, acquires from him indirectly a knowledge of books and half-consciously transmutes the imagery of the Church into the mundane world: 'I imagined that I bore my chalice safely through a throng of foes' (*D* 31). The art of religion is already becoming the religion of art. References to the mass in many of the stories reinforce this association since they are used by Joyce for his own non-ecclesiastical purposes. The first and third stories suggest reasons for Joyce's refusal to enter the priesthood, reasons which anticipate those offered obliquely by Stephen in the *Portrait*. 'The Sisters' and 'Araby' also anticipate Stephen's turning from ecclesiastical forms to aesthetic and emotional experience.

Father Flynn dies at the beginning of the first story; Father Butler is eluded by the boys in 'An Encounter'; a nameless priest dies before the third story opens; a fourth priest, his name unknown to the story's protagonist, has left Ireland before the action of 'Eveline' begins. Thereafter the Church and its representatives become less and less effectual, a process which culminates ironically in 'Grace', originally planned as the conclusion to *Dubliners*. Only in 'The Sisters' and 'Grace', which would have flanked the collection as Joyce envisaged it for several years, are approximations of actual church services depicted. Representatives of the Church are also associated in *Dubliners* with sexual ambivalence or perversity; Father Flynn's relationship with the boy in 'The Sisters' has appeared perverse to many readers and the literary tastes of the priest in 'Araby' call his morality into question.

Thus the priesthood in *Dubliners* seems degenerate and increasingly ineffectual, despite the hold the Church claims to have over the populace. The progressive removal of the priesthood from the centre of the action in the stories intriguingly parallels the retreat of the 'Joycean' narrator. This narrator is most fully present in 'The Sisters' which is largely about a priest and most completely absent in 'Grace' which depicts a priest who has become extremely worldly.

'The Dead', in this area as in much else, is a special case; but, interestingly, Gabriel Conroy, the most 'Joycean' figure in *Dubliners* (at least in the last twelve stories) is present at the party while his brother, a priest, is absent.

These references to European travel, writing and the priesthood are the largest and most conspicuous bases for Joyce's wry comparisons between himself and his characters. There are numerous less prominent examples. One is the connection between the aesthetic Joyce devised at this time, with its emphasis on the nature of beauty and the banal examples of beauty cited by his characters (for example, the appetite-dominated hungry Hungarian Villona in 'After the Race'). Another is the association between Joyce's assumption of a pseudonym ('Stephen Daedalus') to sign the first story and the boys' assumption of false identities ('Murphy' and 'Smith') at the end of the second.

Some of these examples will seem to be grace notes or private jokes. But Joyce was capable of conveying meaning in such ways, as is generally accepted in the case of *Ulysses*, which has been picked over more thoroughly for clues. Whether he expected his strategies to be noticed remains a difficult question, one which currently-fashionable critical methods, with their wariness about authorial intention, can usually evade. It needs to be asked whether Joyce's personal references reinforce meanings present in the text in other forms as well. Where they do so, as in the examples cited above, they may be accepted as part of the texture of the work. The personal references illustrate the intricacy of Joyce's manner of self-definition and imply that with *Dubliners* as with *Finnegans Wake* he wants his book to resemble him.

Thus Joyce uses several of the repeated images of *Dubliners* for the purpose of characterisation. But he also employs for the same purpose particular techniques which appear in only one or two of the stories.

'Eveline', the shortest story and one of the simplest – on the surface – has important autobiographical content and is based on Joyce's self-reflection to a greater extent than has been pointed out. At the same time particular autobiographical connections have been made which do not stand close examination, such as the equation of Frank with Joyce and Eveline with Nora.[5]

It seems clear that Eveline's most immediate living model was Joyce's sister Margaret.[6] The name Eveline Hill echoes Margaret Joyce as Malachi Mulligan ('two dactyls', *U* 4) echoes Oliver Gogarty. Margaret was called Poppie by her family, while Eveline is called Poppens by her suitor. Eveline's nickname seems slightly less intimate than Margaret's, more jolly, more likely to be bestowed on her by a young man than by her relations. It also evokes a doll-like or puppet-like quality about Eveline, a characteristic which reflects on her relationship with Frank. Eveline is the age Margaret reached shortly before the time of the story's composition in 1904, just as Stephen and Bloom in *Ulysses* will share Joyce's own age in the phases of his life he uses them to inspect. In 1904 Margaret, like Eveline, had a dead mother and a drunken and bad-tempered father from whom she had to extract money to buy provisions for the household. Stanislaus reports that 'my sister's main difficulty was to get any money from my father' (*MBK* 239), a phrase which closely echoes the story. Stanislaus has even revealed that John Joyce, like Eveline's father, carried a 'blackthorn stick' (*MBK* 44). Both girls were responsible for the care of young children.

Margaret had played the Joyce piano, whose sale during 1904 upset Joyce and anticipates the 'broken harmonium' in the story. Joyce could have changed a sold piano to a broken harmonium to make more explicit the implications of broken harmony which the piano's fate had symbolised for him. Coincidentally, Margaret had played Eve in the childhood theatricals in which Stanislaus appeared as Adam and James as Satan (*MBK* 3); though it is of course more likely that Joyce named Eveline ironically — an Eve thoroughly intimidated by her father, lacking the courage to pose serious temptation and unwilling to 'fall'. She also looks back to a state of childhood innocence but has nothing with which to replace it.

At the time of writing Joyce was contemplating departure from Ireland for the third time. He was enjoying — mostly — the early days of Nora's company and using his appreciation of Nora's qualities to reinforce his feelings of superiority to his family: 'I told my sister about you last night. It was very amusing', he wrote to Nora (*L II* 50). The Joyce family might seem trapped (and Eveline's family name, Hill, suggests immobility, especially when contrasted with the family of Waters who have 'gone back to England'), but Joyce could distinguish himself by embarking on a relationship with Nora, of whom his family could be expected to disapprove and by leaving home. 'We were seventeen in family. My brothers and sisters are nothing to me. One brother alone is capable of understanding me', he told Nora (*L II* 48). Joyce no doubt envisaged that brother, Stanislaus, playing a major role in *Stephen Hero*, where (as Maurice Daedalus) he would serve as a foil and a sounding-board for Stephen/Joyce. While Stanislaus is a model for James Duffy in 'A Painful Case', no trace of him appears in any of the homes in *Dubliners* which reflect the Joyce household; the boy narrators in the first three stories, for example, seem to lack siblings as well as parents. Joyce changes his companion in the adventure narrated in the second story from his brother to a friend.

With Stanislaus already reserved for use in *Stephen Hero*, then, Joyce would logically turn to Margaret as a member of his family who could represent entrapment in Dublin. She would be treated with compassion but also aloofness ('My brothers and sisters are nothing to me'); she would be smothered in family and she would turn down an opportunity to leave Dublin. (Soon after the story was written Margaret tried to dissuade Joyce from leaving Ireland with Nora; in this way, as in others, the story is oddly prophetic.) Joyce often associated the image of drowning, mentioned at the end of 'Eveline', with the fear of being smothered by one's family. Stephen thinks of his sister in *Ulysses*: 'She is drowning. . . . She will drown me with her, eyes and hair. Lank coils of seaweed hair around me, my heart, my soul. Salt green death' (*U* 243).

In 1904 it must have seemed possible that Eveline, having failed to leave with Frank, would become a nun. By 1910 Margaret Joyce had in fact become a nun and this change may have prompted Joyce, revising the story for an edition which was supposed to appear in that year, to add the reference to Blessed Margaret Mary Alacoque, the most substantial revision he made at this time. Margaret Mary is associated with Eveline Hill and links her to Margaret Joyce who was to become, perhaps by a fortunate coincidence, Sister Mary Gertrude. Eveline is a debased Margaret Mary whose vision of the Sacred Heart she recalls only in her 'palpitations', an affliction which symbolises her emotional instability, her denial of the sacredness of the heart, of the central importance of love. But while Margaret Joyce, in becoming a nun, had 'escaped' to New Zealand, Eveline — despite the curiously prophetic flight of the priest to Melbourne, already present in the 1904 version of the story — would remain trapped in Dublin.

The suggestion, already mentioned, that Joyce presents himself as Frank and Nora as Eveline, requires correction. Frank does share with Joyce his yachting cap, overseas experience, fondness for singing and relationship with a young woman in Dublin. But the differences are much more striking. Frank shows no sign of any literary interests, even by the standards of the characters of *Dubliners*; it is difficult to imagine him writing Eveline a letter. He lacks, as far as we can tell, Joyce's kind of religious and family context (whereas the boy in 'The Sisters', though he seems to lack parents, lives with an aunt and uncle clearly based on Joyce's parents). After Frank returns to his native country he lodges not with family but in 'a house on the main road'. 'Frankness' is the opposite of 'silence, exile and cunning', a credo Joyce was already formulating. Frank strikes Eveline as 'very kind, manly, open-hearted', all attributes which induced some scepticism in Joyce; they are the kinds of values wrongly attributed by people like Simon Dedalus to environments like schools. Where the word 'frank' appears elsewhere in *Dubliners*, except in 'The Dead', it is generally ironical (see, for example, *D* 64, 174). Frank's idea of overseas experience is that of the adventurer, like Mahony in 'An Encounter', rather than the dedicated seeker of broader knowledge. He has chosen to live in Buenos Aires and has been to Patagonia and Canada: all in the New World, the Americas, which Joyce instinctively disliked and never visited.

Besides being a place to which Irish people did emigrate and a Catholic city Buenos Aires seems an altogether too appropriate scene for Eveline's projected 'new life'; the 'good air' its name evokes contrasts with the dusty air of Dublin, where Eveline will remain, perhaps also with the 'melancholy air' of Italy (a phrase used in the story) which would be more to Joyce's taste. (Compare with Buenos Aires Melbourne, a 'better place', a 'new port'. Incidentally 'going to Buenos Aires' was once a common euphemism for 'becoming a prostitute'.)[7] Frank, having 'fallen on his feet' (*D* 39), provides a pedestrian travesty of Stephen's sense of his destiny as one who will 'fall' in the *Portrait*. Frank seems to suffer from delusions — surely his image of Eveline as a suitable wife for him is a fantasy — while Joyce, already, takes present reality as his province. Frank thus appears as a mock-Joyce, scarcely closer to him than Lenehan was.

Nor is Eveline much like Nora. Eveline remains static and passive, finally reacting like a terrified caged animal to the prospect of elopement with Frank, clutching at the iron rail in her anguish, as later Mrs Sinico will die on iron rails. (The 'sudden failure of the heart's action' which causes Mrs Sinico's death is a more extreme version of Eveline's palpitations and like them suggests emotional problems. In Mrs Sinico's case it seems to be Duffy's heart which has failed to act.) By contrast with Eveline's panic, Nora is depicted by Ellmann 'sauntering' about Dublin and into Joyce's life (*JJ* 159) and the spirited Galway girl bears little resemblance to the enervated Eveline who has always lived in Dublin. As Joyce and Nora contemplated departure for Europe, Nora 'was too much like a girl going off to summer camp, and he tried to make clear to her how reckless and drastic a step they were taking' (*JJ* 177). Their positions here are far from those shown in the story. It could even be argued that Joyce bestows Nora's high spirits on Frank and transfers his own anxiety to Eveline.

Autobiographical characterisation in 'Eveline', then, is mostly a matter of contrast. Joyce presents the image of a man who, while amusingly resembling him in appearance, is quite different in spirit, incapable of his own understanding or purposiveness. He presents, too, an image of his family as they were after he had left them, with a scene in which he imagines his eldest sister rejecting a suitor who might have rescued her. 'Eveline' is a sad story and its melancholy is firmly based in Joyce's personal musings. The story dramatises his estrangement from his family by showing how superior he himself was to the kind of image of escape his family might be able to envisage and how in the end they could not embrace even that.

In 'Eveline', therefore, Joyce makes himself the oblique measure of his subject, contrasting characters and events in the story with what he felt his own circumstances to be.

Similar strategies can be seen operating in many of the other stories, of which the most interesting is 'The Dead'. When Joyce added 'The Dead' to *Dubliners*, no doubt he was partly seeking, as he said, to put the record straight by illustrating Dublin's hospitality and warmth, slighted in most of the earlier stories. He also showed concern with the shape of the whole collection, a concern apparent in some of the parallels between this last story and the first. 'The Dead' contains a prominent pair of sisters, as 'The Sisters' had been much concerned with a dead man. 'The Sisters' begins with a boy looking in through a window and wondering whether the man inside is alive or dead, while 'The Dead' ends with a man looking out through a window, meditating on the image of a dying boy which his wife has just described for him and envisaging some dissolution or fusing of both living and dead. But in addition to such corrections of emphasis and structural felicities, Joyce may also have wished to end the volume by making a more personal appearance. The last few stories before 'The Dead' show a kind of progressive effacement of the author, anticipating Stephen's prescriptions for this process given in the *Portrait*; but in 'The Dead' Joyce appears with an immediacy not seen since the first three stories of the volume (the first of which, along with two later ones — 'Eveline' and 'After the Race' — had initially appeared over the name of Stephen Daedalus).

One such 'more personal appearance' may lurk in the photograph Gabriel sees depicting his mother and brother. In this photograph his mother 'held an open book on her knees and was pointing out something in it to Constantine who, dressed in a man-o'-war suit, lay at her feet' (*D* 186). This sounds suspiciously like a description of an actual photograph and a glance at the picture taken to show Joyce with his parents and grandfather, just before he began school, confirms the suspicion.[8]

Gabriel Conroy is the most immediately and conspicuously Joycean protagonist in the later stories. His resemblances to Joyce are well-known: his physical appearance, Continental experience and enthusiasms, teaching, book-reviewing and relationship with a woman from Galway who had had an admirer named Michael. Gabriel and Joyce also have affinities in personality; Gabriel's fears resemble Joyce's and anticipate aspects of Richard Rowan in *Exiles* and of Bloom in *Ulysses*. Gabriel's relationship with his aunts evokes Joyce's changing attitudes to his family at the time he wrote the story. There is still reserve and a fear of stagnation or entrapment (the aunts' family name, Morkan, is suggestive: a 'morkin' is literally 'a beast which dies by disease or accident'). Yet there is also a new compassion in the relationship and a new self-scrutiny in which superiority could not be glibly assumed. For most of the story Gabriel treats his aunts urbanely.

Joyce's concern with the power of the dead over the living — a prominent theme throughout *Dubliners*, culminating in 'The Dead' — must owe something to his brooding on his mother's death, still a recent memory when the stories were written. Several of Joyce's characters, both in *Dubliners* and elsewhere, have to contend with the memories of mothers who had restricted them when alive and who dominate their thoughts once dead (Eveline Hill, Gabriel Conroy, Richard Rowan, and Stephen in *Ulysses*, for example). For Eveline, 'the pitiful vision of her mother's life laid its spell on the very quick of her being' (*D* 40), a mild anticipation of the power of Stephen's mother over him in *Ulysses*: 'Her glazing eyes, staring out of death, to shake and bend my soul. On me alone. The ghostcandle to light her agony. Ghostly light on the tortured face. . . . Her eyes on me to strike me down' (*U* 10). Gabriel remembers his mother's 'sullen opposition to his marriage' (*D* 187), a resentment he shares with Richard Rowan.

Gabriel thinks of his mother's opposition to his marriage immediately after reflecting on pictures of the balcony scene in *Romeo and Juliet* and of the murdered princes in the tower — a play and an historical incident both depicting young love or leadership smothered by an older generation. But when in his speech Gabriel says of the Morkans 'I will not attempt to play to-night the part that Paris played on another occasion. I will not attempt to choose between them' (*D* 204), he might remind us that in Greek mythology Paris awarded the beauty prize to Aphrodite; Gabriel's failure to choose could be interpreted as a failure to recognise what Aphrodite represents — the true nature of love.

The conjunction of the *Romeo and Juliet* reference and the allusion to Paris also suggests a parallel with the Paris who appears in the play: the unsuccessful third member of a love triangle, which is how Gabriel will regard himself in his moment of self-reproach after Gretta's revelation about Michael Furey. The image of Michael standing under Gretta's window recalls the balcony scene in the play, again suggesting that Michael might be the true lover and Gabriel (as Paris) the stuffy unsuccessful suitor. These allusions seem at first to limit Gabriel. But they also reflect his own ability to apply literary contexts to his situation, to attain a broader sense of connection between people than most characters in *Dubliners* are able to perceive. We should not take Gabriel's own remorse at the end of the story too seriously. It is a more positive emotion than it seems because it reflects his sensitivity, his willingness to acknowledge the effects he has on other people's lives. Gabriel, uniquely in the collection, is given the benefit of Joyce's mature, self-critical perspective and he thus moves *Dubliners* away from the hostility and alienation which mark many of the earlier stories, in a direction of relative harmony.

Thus the autobiographical content of 'The Dead' concerns more than Joyce's self-analysis or the Michael Bodkin/Michael Furey connection. More immediately, we see Joyce stepping back into *Dubliners*, ensuring that the final image of the city relates personally to him. The partial escape from egotism which Gabriel manages at the end of the story has parallels in Joyce's writing life as well. 'The Dead' was written just as Joyce was deciding to rework *Stephen Hero* into *A Portrait of the Artist as a Young Man*. Those two titles imply and the books confirm that the later Stephen will be presented more humbly, less heroically and with more qualifications than the earlier one.

Moreover, with the addition of 'The Dead' *Dubliners* comes to embody in its total movement the structure which binds together all of Joyce's works. Images of the isolated individual give way to images of the society surrounding that individual, to be followed in turn by a combined image in which the individual fits, however uncomfortably, into his social context. This union between the self and the world parallels the image of qualified unity conveyed at the end of 'The Dead' in the scene where Gretta is asleep and Gabriel lies awake thinking before going to sleep himself. *Ulysses, Exiles* and *Finnegans Wake* will end similarly, with one member of a couple awake thinking while the other rests or sleeps. This parallel with later works again recalls the fact that as he wrote 'The Dead' Joyce planned to recast *Stephen Hero* into the *Portrait*, which would become a kind of sequel and counterweight to *Dubliners*. A structure had been worked out in a sequence of stories within one book — *Dubliners* — and could now be explored more fully in a succession of separate books treating the same stages with increasing detail and subtlety.

中文

3

A Portrait of the Artist as a Young Man

Joyce's various works bear crucial relationships to each other, a fact he emphasised by insisting that *Ulysses* should not be translated into a particular language unless the *Portrait* had already appeared in that language: the one work is essential to the other and the sequence between them must be preserved. Such relationships between works particularly affect Joyce's most directly autobiographical character, Stephen Dedalus.

The path from *Dubliners* to the *Portrait* makes a detour through *Stephen Hero*, the incomplete draft of an autobiographical novel. It resembles *Dubliners* in tone and method, particularly in its passages of social commentary. As in the stories, frequent attacks are made on conformity and intellectual timidity. Specific satiric targets include the priesthood, which again appears as sexually indeterminate and sleepy: the College President has the smile of a 'pretty girl' (*SH* 90) and makes 'a slow hermaphroditic gesture' (*SH* 98); the lay-brother who 'roused himself from a stupefied doze in expectation of silver' (*SH* 119) recalls the priest in 'The Sisters'.

Stephen Hero also has an engaging immediacy, resulting partly from its rough-hewn unfinished texture, which helps us to measure the detachment Joyce achieved later. This version of Stephen receives a less rigorous artistic shaping than his later counterparts in the *Portrait* and *Ulysses* and consequently seems artless, naive, lifelike in his inadequacies and in the random nature of his experiences. He displays some inconsistencies and some commonplace preoccupations which will not figure in the *Portrait* and parts of the manuscript seem by Joyce's later standards unselfconscious and even flabby, as in this account of one of Stephen's pastimes: 'Another favourite [game] was "Who's Who." A person goes out of the room and the rest of the company choose the name of someone who is supposed to have special attractions for the absent player' (*SH* 45). Of course, Joyce would have removed many such passages in revision, as in fact he did in writing the *Portrait* but *Stephen Hero* retains its own interest as a distinct stage in Joyce's literary transmutation of his experiences.

It would be a mistake to see in *Stephen Hero* a direct expression of Joyce's view of his past. Yet *Stephen Hero* is héld back from such 'honesty' less by an achieved fictive detachment than by a facetiousness — even disingenuousness — concerning the importance of Stephen's life. Joyce has not yet decided how seriously to take his hero, or how seriously the reader should take him. It seems that Stephen's activities must be significant, or there would be no reason to record them; but he is frequently undercut by explicit mockery, as when he appears as a 'heaven-ascending essayist' or a 'fiery-hearted revolutionary' (*SH* 80). We believe neither that Stephen deserves such epithets in fact, nor that Joyce thinks he does. It is as if Stephen's own adolescent callowness and insecurity contaminate the text in which he appears. Yet at the same time there is obviously present a narrator who is not Stephen. Stephen and his views are sometimes treated in a raw, awkward, joking manner, a manner which also appears in Joyce's letters from time to time. This comparison suggests that Stephen's persona has not yet been fully imagined. As Hugh Kenner has remarked, Joyce writes clumsily when he has not imagined a persona through whom he can communicate, a situation which arises most often in letters. 'When Joyce was unsure of his role words swarmed in his head but all syntactic sense deserted him. Syntax was a function of role: of character.'[1] And not syntax alone but also the tone and manner which syntax helps to convey.

This early version of Stephen, while more immediate and likeable than the *Portrait* version, is thus less consistent and realised with less imagination. *Stephen Hero* is impressive at moments — especially in its recorded conversations, when authorial tone is less crucial — but is not sufficiently consistent in purpose to convey the development of a character. Its lack of any beginning (because part of the manuscript has been lost, probably discarded by Joyce when he had quarried the material for the *Portrait*) or ending (because Joyce never did finish writing it, but began work on the *Portrait* instead) seems appropriate; *Stephen Hero* has jagged edges and shades into real life at both ends, never attaining a unified or distinct form. It could be said that Joyce achieved a milder but more deliberate version of the same effect through the fragmentary first and last scenes of the *Portrait*. Stephen seems to make little progress during the work, not because there is a pattern of advances and retreats, as there is in the *Portrait*, but because of these stylistic and structural traits. Perhaps *Stephen Hero* suffers from the same problems as Stephen's paper 'Drama and Life', which is mentioned in it: Stephen 'had occupied himself so much with securing the foundations that he had not left himself space enough to raise the complete structure' (*SH* 81). The *Dubliners*-based method of external observation suffices for the 'foundations' of a self-portrait but the 'complete structure' will require a new technique.

For the *Portrait* itself Joyce makes his material tauter and more consistent. He introduces the mimetic method by which the development of the novel's style is tied closely to Stephen's evolving consciousness and seems to grow out of it, a method which may owe something to the progressive tracing of different consciousnesses through different styles in *Dubliners*. He pares away Stephen's family background, so that we concentrate on the central character; and he removes much other material not directly relevant to his central concerns. Joyce retreats into the 'enigma of a manner' (*SH* 27) as the explicitness of *Stephen Hero* gives way to a cryptic novel in which the author is much harder to find and in which nothing is elucidated, all is presented dramatic-ally — a pattern which Joyce would follow in all his later works. Some of the associations between phases of Stephen's experience are extremely sly. Mr Tate's accusation that Stephen has 'heresy in his essay' (*P* 79) is foreshadowed by the phrasing (though not the literal circumstances) of Father Dolan's question to Stephen, 'Why are you not writing *like the others?'* (*P* 49, emphasis added). Both accusations seek to make a norm of conformity, especially conformity in writing: an ironic anticipation of Joyce's career as a writer who never tried to conform.

One function of this change from *Stephen Hero* to the *Portrait* is to make Joyce's relationship to Stephen more inscrutable. In *Stephen Hero* the relationship fluctuates between extremes, combining warm endorsement with occasional icy scepticism. Both extreme tones are muted in the *Portrait*, where Joyce has caused critics like Wayne Booth apparently endless consternation by refusing to pass explicit judgment on Stephen (though why such judgment should be expected, after Joyce had already portrayed characters like Maria and Gabriel Conroy with a balance of positive and negative evaluative possibilities, is not clear). The title *Stephen Hero* must have come to appear too unequivocal; the new title *A Portrait of the Artist as a Young Man* introduces greater neutrality, some qualification ('as a young man', a phrase Joyce stressed in conversation) and hints of an autobiographical association between author and character — hints which are never insisted on or directly supported in the text even though all readers must now know the connection to exist.

The new Stephen is a more independent being than his predecessor in *Stephen Hero*. He may still resemble Joyce closely but he is nevertheless more detached from him. In *Stephen Hero* Joyce does not always bother to write as if Stephen were someone other than himself; in fact, there are frequent suggestions otherwise, in the form of diary-like narrative and outbursts of sympathy and indignation. In the *Portrait* Joyce does write as if Stephen is someone apart from himself. More than that, he writes as if the relationship between author and character no longer interests him. This detachment and apparent indifference accord with the tone and meaning of the novel: these are qualities which Stephen himself seeks as he removes himself progressively from his background and environment. Again, the diary in the *Portrait* lacks the immediacy of the diary-like sections of *Stephen Hero*; it is mannered, literary, very much Stephen's own self-conscious work. Stephen reflects rather pompously, for example, that 'the past is consumed in the present and the present is living only because it brings forth the future' (*P* 251). Self-directed humour and irony show the perfection of a manner, rather than any real immediacy achieved (or, perhaps, sought) by either Stephen or Joyce: 'O, give it up, old chap! Sleep it off!' (*P* 252).

It is also worth remembering that between *Stephen Hero* and the *Portrait* Stephen's surname changes from Daedalus to Dedalus. This change moves him away, however slightly, from a classical prototype, so that he appears more convincingly as a character in his own right: his name still determines his nature, but not so completely. The new name, if still 'absurd . . . an ancient Greek' (*U* 3), is slightly more plausible for a citizen of modern Europe. Stephen's experiences are more selectively treated, also, in the later novel; we only see in detail those moments which Stephen deems to be important. The effect of this emphasis resembles that of his new name: he becomes more independent, less predetermined; not a series of experiences, or a means for Joyce to make a series of points but a character with a distinct personality of his own.

In the *Portrait*, Joyce writes about Stephen from a later position of strength and some literary achievements. 'The Dead' is the most impressive of these, but as relevant here is *Stephen Hero* itself, a text which also acts as a buffer between the Joyce now writing and the experiences he describes. Stephen's experiences in the *Portrait*, we imagine, are in many cases drawn not from life but from *Stephen Hero*. There is thus less need for the uncertainty and nervous humour often present in the earlier work. The distinction is clearer in the *Portrait* between the creative mature artist and the younger potential artist, whereas in *Stephen Hero* both were still potential artists. The connection between himself and the persona thus occupies the writer less than before and so he can adopt a more relaxed, detached and enigmatic tone in which that connection seems to be the least of his worries.

Readers, assuming that Stephen is an approximate copy of Joyce, are also likely to take the connection for granted. Believing that the events of the *Portrait* 'really' happened, they will not query the plot, the succession of Stephen's experiences, but assume that the novel simply traces Joyce's own past.

It has also been assumed in criticism that Stephen's character is extrapolated from Joyce's at each point in his development; that while there may be differences between them, continuity is provided by a centripetal effect which repeatedly brings Stephen back to the Joycean position after he has erred from it. This view perhaps gains implicit support from the novel's pulsating structure which suggests that Stephen is continually recalled to a central position.

Yet it is also possible that Joyce attempted to imagine Stephen as a distinct character and pursued the attributes bestowed on him to their logical conclusions. Such was certainly not the case in *Stephen Hero* – hence, partly, the discontinuity of that Stephen's personality. If the Stephen of the *Portrait* undergoes a more consistent and plausible development, seems to be presented chiefly in terms of those attributes which we can watch maturing, we should admit the possibility that this effect owes something to Joyce's skill in constructing the character, not merely to the continuity of Joyce's own life. In the early essay 'A Portrait of the Artist', Joyce discusses the continuity of personality:

> The features of infancy are not commonly reproduced in the adolescent portrait for, so capricious are we, that we cannot or will not conceive the past in any other than its iron, memorial aspect. Yet the past assuredly implies a fluid succession of presents, the development of an entity of which our actual present is a phase only. Our world, again, recognises its acquaintance chiefly by the characters of beard and inches and is, for the most part, estranged from those of its members who seek through some art, by some process of the mind as yet untabulated, to liberate from the personalised lumps of matter that which is their individuating rhythm, the first or formal relation of their parts. But for such as these a portrait is not an identificative paper but rather the curve of an emotion (*P* 257–8).

Stephen Hero and the novel *Portrait* have some of their origins in this essay and apparently are meant to manifest a similar notion of character-development. Stanislaus noted that in *Stephen Hero* Joyce thought of a man's character as developing 'from an embryo with constant traits' (*MBK* 17). But only the *Portrait* successfully shows a character changing consistently in his own terms.

Accounts of Joyce's early life – notably those provided by Stanislaus and by Richard Ellmann – confirm a few distinctions between Joyce and Stephen. What we will be seeking here is the continuity to be found among those attributes of Stephen which are not drawn directly from Joyce's life.

Stanislaus has disclosed some particularly surprising differences between author and character. He may have exaggerated some of these, as his own contribution to literature or in over-reaction to popular misconceptions (and, perhaps, overlooking in the process ways in which Stephen may have been based on himself as well as on Joyce). Nonetheless, we must accept his statement that Joyce as a schoolboy was more athletic and popular than Stephen seems to be. By careful selection of incident, Joyce shows Stephen's schooldays, particularly at Clongowes, as times of travail. Throughout the first school scene (*P* 8–27) Stephen is ill, having caught a chill after being 'shouldered ... into the square ditch the day before' (*P* 14). Throughout the second school scene (*P* 40–59) he has inadequate vision, because 'a sprinter had knocked him down the day before ... and his spectacles had been broken in three pieces' (*P* 41). Joyce no doubt had moments of illness or weakness at school. The point is that Stephen suffers in these ways throughout the time we see him at Clongowes: he is knocked down twice, feverish, unable to see properly. (Novel characters have only the continuity we intuit in them and we can only extrapolate from what we are shown.)

The moment of exultation after Stephen's appeal to authority at the end of the first chapter (later undercut by the revelation of the rector's light-hearted duplicity, *P* 72) and Stephen's attempts at running under the tutelage of the decrepit Mike Flynn scarcely modify this impression which has been made forcefully at the outset: 'He felt his body small and weak amid the throng of players and his eyes were weak and watery' (*P* 8). It is not stated explicitly that Stephen dislikes athletics, but the implication is there; for example: 'The coming of September did not trouble him this year for he was not to be sent back to Clongowes. The practice in the park came to an end when Mike Flynn went into hospital' (*P* 63–4).

Further discrepancies between author and character follow. Stanislaus reports that Joyce found it easy to laugh at – or with – his father's various and numerous social indiscretions, while Stephen is deeply troubled by his father's errant ways. This discrepancy must have struck Stanislaus with particular force, since it is at this point in his narration that he adds the remark 'Stephen Dedalus is an imaginary, not a real, self-portrait and freely treated' (*MBK* 48). Stanislaus also states that 'for the character of Stephen in both drafts of the novel [that is, in both *Stephen Hero* and the *Portrait*] he has followed his own development closely, been his own model and chosen to use many incidents from his own experience, but he has transformed and invented many others' (*MBK* 17). Stanislaus doubts that Joyce's visit to Cork with his father produced the raw misery Stephen feels when he makes the trip, for 'my brother's letters home at the time were written in a tone of amusement even when he described going from one bar to another' (*MBK* 60). The 'tone of amusement' could have been partly bravado, but the suspicion that this visit did not disturb Joyce as much as it disturbs Stephen is consistent with our other impressions of the two father-son relationships. Ellmann comments further that 'in *A Portrait* Stephen denies that Simon is in any real sense his father, but James himself had no doubt that he was in every way his father's son' (*JJ* 22). Young Stephen seems to lack the self-insight or sense of humour which enabled Joyce from an early age to acknowledge a strong sense of kinship with his egotistic, articulate, improvident father.

It seems likely that Stephen's fellow-students who converse with him in the final chapter are 'reduced' versions of their living models. They may bear vestigial scars from *Stephen Hero*, where Stephen's associates regularly serve as targets of the narrator's ridicule. Ellmann notes that Joyce's friend Skeffington appears as McCann in the *Portrait* and is 'a little absurd, a less agile debater in fiction than he was in fact' (*JJ* 62). Surviving manuscripts suggest that Joyce's friend and enemy Oliver Gogarty was to appear in the *Portrait*, but he has been edited out of the novel by the removal of what would presumably have been its final scene. Gogarty would have been a formidable antagonist for Stephen — as he proves to be in *Ulysses* when he appears as Buck Mulligan.[2] The effect of these attenuations and suppressions is that Stephen has to face milder and less serious opposition from his contemporaries than Joyce did; also, Stephen's isolation is intensified as there seems to be nobody with whom he can communicate successfully. Thus his ideas seem less tested, more fragile and more peculiar to himself than Joyce's. Kevin Sullivan notes that 'what Dedalus mirrors, and that only imperfectly, is the cerebral, self-conscious, and self-defeating aspects of the Joyce original'.[3] This emphasis is particularly clear in Stephen's relations with his contemporaries.

These examples denote an attempt by Joyce to make Stephen rather less successful, cheerful and well-adjusted than he himself had been. There is an approximate continuity among those aspects of Stephen which most strikingly fail to correspond closely to Joyce's life. Mostly they disclose inadequacies in Stephen's relations with his peers or with his father. Stephen is a weaker child, less capable of filial esteem or sympathy and less given to camaraderie than Joyce. Rather than being set up by contrast with Joyce from time to time these features do seem to be functions of the personality Stephen is given at the outset. While Joyce tried to make some people about whom he wrote — such as William Blake — resemble him more closely than in fact they did, he clearly shows Stephen as less like himself than he could have been and tries to give him some consistency in his own terms.

Thus Joyce not only keeps his persona at arm's length, he also contrives to give the persona unity and continuity independent of his own personality and development. We need now to decide on the purposes of this strategy.

First, the method reminds us that in a sense the novel is Stephen's own. He derives a kind of authority from his apparently independent existence. Nothing which happens in the novel takes place outside Stephen's area of awareness. The obvious contrast here is with *Ulysses*, where much occurs of which Stephen is unaware. It can be argued (and will be later) that some of Joyce's ironies of emphasis are not for Stephen's eyes, but this argument does not affect the point that all the novel's events are accessible to Stephen. There is thus a sense in which Stephen, as a character who is not Joyce, 'creates' the novel – in that it only exists as a record of the distinct individual, Stephen Dedalus and his responses to experience. This strategy gives the novel both a wry detachment and a unity of focus.

Second, the novel concerns Stephen's attempt to shape an identity for himself and he could not be permitted to shape one indistinguishable from Joyce's. Joyce wanted to study the creation of a self using a kindred but not identical persona, so that the self could be seen to be created, not simply to follow a path Joyce had already taken. Stephen's volition – never impressively strong in any case – might seem impossibly attenuated if his development were a mere recapitulation of Joyce's life.

Third, the method allows Joyce to hide from view, when it suits him, partly because Stephen is not himself and partly because only Joyce knows exactly to what extent and in what circumstances this is true. If this method had not been available to him it is likely that Joyce would have found it difficult to write autobiographically at all. The strategy seems necessary to allow Joyce to write the account of his past which, at this stage of his career, he evidently felt obliged to write.

One function of this delicately balanced Stephen is to evolve a view of art in a way which illustrates the growth of intellectual positions from experience and to demonstrate Joyce's view of how this process occurs. Joyce's own aesthetic opinions and his experience differ from Stephen's in many details but what interests him is the nature of the relationship between experience and belief. Stephen's aesthetic, which he expounds in the final chapter of the *Portrait*, bears an interesting relationship to the events of Stephen's past life.

In his conversation with Lynch Stephen concerns himself with the definition of pity and terror; with the dismissal of improper, kinetic art (propaganda and pornography) whose aim is to excite loathing or desire; with the nature of the beauty which proper art expresses; with the 'wholeness, harmony and radiance' which he sees as necessary to aesthetic apprehension; and with the lyric, epic and dramatic phases of art. In the dramatic phase, he says, 'the artist, like the God of the creation, remains within or behind or beyond or above his handiwork, invisible, refined out of existence, indifferent, paring his fingernails' (*P* 215). Art, Stephen says, is 'the human disposition of sensible or intelligible matter for an esthetic end' (*P* 207).

These ideas have antecedents, acknowledged by Stephen, in Aristotle and Aquinas and others unacknowledged by Stephen in Wilde and Ruskin (not to mention Joyce). But they also owe much to Stephen's own experiences. Terror and pity, for example, preoccupy Stephen in his recollection of his earliest years. We recall Stephen's 'terrorstricken face' (*P* 39) after the Christmas dinner scene; when he is pandied at Clongowes 'his whole body was shaking with fright' (*P* 50) and afterwards 'Stephen knelt down quickly pressing his beaten hands to his sides. To think of them beaten and swollen with pain all in a moment made him feel so sorry for them as if they were not his own but someone else's that he felt sorry for' (*P* 51). Terror and pity are aroused again by the sermon in the third chapter and Stephen's response to it.

Desire and loathing are also preoccupations of Stephen's young life. Sexual desire and the self-contempt Stephen associates with it dominate Chapter 2 and determine Stephen's state of mind at the retreat in Chapter 3:

> From the evil seed of lust all other deadly sins had sprung forth: pride in himself and contempt of others, covetousness in using money for the purchase of unlawful pleasure, envy of those whose vices he could not reach to and calumnious murmuring against the pious, gluttonous enjoyment of food, the dull glowering anger amid which he brooded upon his longing, the swamp of spiritual and bodily sloth in which his whole being had sunk (*P* 106).

Stephen's explanation of why the 'kinetic' arts are improper, though we may agree with his conclusion, is in itself cyclic and unconvincing. It seems much more plausible that he himself wants to escape from desire and loathing into a detached and contemplative life as he does, to some extent, in announcing his aesthetic. It is also true, however, that the sermons in Chapter 3 are highly kinetic in Stephen's sense and may help to explain his opposition to this form of discourse or art.

Ugliness and beauty preoccupy Stephen at the end of Chapter 4. His sense of destiny forms as he contrasts his swimming schoolmates with the birdgirl. The schoolmates are ugly adolescents and remind him of his own awkwardness: 'It was a pain to see them and a swordlike pain to see the signs of adolescence that made repellent their pitiable naked-ness. . . . But he, apart from them and in silence, remembered in what dread he stood of the mystery of his own body' (*P* 168). The birdgirl, on the other hand, 'seemed like one whom magic had changed into the likeness of a strange and beautiful seabird' (*P* 171).

The fifth chapter begins with a vision of ugliness and resulting contempt.[4] Stephen, hearing the mad nun screech-ing, 'shook the sound out of his ears by an angry toss of his head and hurried on, stumbling through the mouldering offal, his heart already bitten by an ache of loathing and bitterness. His father's whistle, his mother's mutterings, the screech of an unseen maniac were to him now so many voices offending and threatening to humble the pride of his youth' (*P* 175-6). Stephen's search for the 'essence of beauty' takes place in and because of these surroundings. He cultivates a detachment from his disordered environment, suppressing reactions of revulsion and strengthening his soul by con-templation, acquiring control over his responses, seeking in art a shapeliness and order which his surroundings fail to provide.

All these experiences — which together constitute most of what has happened to Stephen, or at least most of those significant moments which we have been privileged to witness — relate closely to his aesthetic. Terror and the pity it can evoke have been the extreme emotions of his childhood and adolescence; thus he needs to define and so control them. Having formulated an aesthetic, he is able to experience such emotions in a more voluntary manner. This pattern is clearly expressed in *Stephen Hero*: 'He smiled because it seemed to him so unexpected a ripeness in himself – this pity – or rather this impulse of pity for he had no more than entertained it. But it was the actual achievement of his essay which had allowed him so mature a pleasure as the sensation of pity for another' (*SH* 76). Similarly, desire and loathing have troubled Stephen greatly. By ruling that they are improper material for art – even as he resolves to become an artist – he gains control over them, achieving the kind of 'stasis' he claims art should also produce. Again, his search for beauty is a defence against disorder, an attempt to see the world on his own terms rather than terms chosen by the world. Even before he goes to Belvedere, Stephen's manner of assessing the world takes a form which will be approved in his aesthetic discussion: 'He chronicled with patience what he saw, detaching himself from it and testing its mortifying flavour in secret' (*P* 67).

Stephen's concern with wholeness, harmony and radiance, while closely following Aquinas, also owes something to his search for individuality and detachment from his surroundings. He stresses to Lynch (obviously chosen as a challenging auditor because of his normally extreme insensitivity to aesthetics) the uniqueness of the object of apprehension, the need to see it as 'complex, multiple, divisible, separable, made up of its parts, the result of its parts and their sum, harmonious' (*P* 212) and as possessing its own essence. The same terms could be applied to the self as the object of contemplation or the subject of a work of art. Stephen's concern with his 'difference', which is marked in the *Portrait* and modified in *Ulysses*, accords with this aesthetic; the autobiographical artist writes of himself in the terms Stephen has delineated.

It could also be said that Stephen's personal development follows the lyric-epic-dramatic pattern he describes for literature. The same is true of many people, but the pattern is heightened in the account of Stephen's life which leads up to his announcement of his aesthetic. Stephen's relationship to his experience resembles the artist's relationship to his material, as is particularly appropriate for an autobiographical writer. Lyric is an immediate, unselfconscious form, according to Stephen; the person uttering a lyric cry 'is more conscious of the instant of emotion than of himself as feeling emotion' (*P* 214). This description accords with the Stephen we see in the first chapter. The increasing detachment of the artist from his described experience until the dramatic mode is reached resembles Stephen's increasingly skilful efforts to control the forces acting on him.

Stephen's definition of art stresses conscious control over the act of creation. One of the puzzles which he has set himself and which he reports to Lynch is designed to illustrate this point: 'If a man hacking in fury at a block of wood . . . make there an image of a cow, is that image a work of art? If not, why not?' (*P* 214). The answer to this question can be found in Joyce's aesthetic notebooks but it may in any case be deduced from the context in the *Portrait*: such an image could not be a work of art because it is not a *deliberate* arrangement of matter for an aesthetic end. Stephen would have no time for an artist who believed in unconscious creation, or who thought beauty could be achieved unawares. The artists he admires, such as Ibsen, share his view of the deliberate nature of artistic creation. More importantly, Stephen has to stress these aspects of artistic activity because they are essential to his own careful, conscious methods of coming to terms with life, not only as an artist but as a young man.

One more aspect of Stephen's thought seems to be grounded on his own experience in ways he does not fully understand or acknowledge in the *Portrait*: the notion of epiphanies. This concept is treated quite forcefully during Stephen's aesthetic discussions in *Stephen Hero* but is not directly mentioned in the *Portrait*. By an epiphany Stephen means 'a sudden spiritual manifestation, whether in the vulgarity of speech or of gesture or in a memorable phase of the mind itself' (*SH* 211). It will strike any reader of the *Portrait* that Stephen has indeed experienced life in the form of epiphanies, successive revelations either of external reality or of an aspect of his own being and following a general but not unbroken progress towards truth. In *Stephen Hero* Stephen half-acknowledges the biographical implications of epiphany. Epiphany is the most personal aspect of Stephen's aesthetic theory since an epiphany happens to an individual and must be interpreted by him. Perhaps the need to acknowledge such implications when introducing the notion of epiphany caused Joyce to omit all mention of the idea from the *Portrait*. Thus in the later novel impersonality could be preserved and the explicit connection between Stephen's ideas and experiences could be suppressed.

What Joyce gives us in Stephen's aesthetic, then, is a series of precepts firmly grounded in experience. For us, if not for Stephen's peers, this connection adds both dignity and irony to his thoughts. Dignity, because the thoughts are not spun out of the air but based on actuality; irony, because Stephen does not acknowledge any such connection and because the aesthetic hardly concerns itself with experience at all. Stephen's closest approach to such an acknowledgment comes in this passage, during his discussion with Lynch:

> — We are right, he said, and the others are wrong. To speak of these things and to try to understand their nature and, having understood it, to try slowly and humbly and constantly to express, to press out again, from the gross earth or what it brings forth, from sound and shape and colour which are the prison gates of our soul, an image of the beauty we have come to understand — that is art (*P* 206–7).

Even this formulation, impressive as far as it goes, overlooks the real function of experience in the creation of art.

This irony is at Stephen's expense, but like much of the irony in the *Portrait* it does not aim to repudiate him. It has two functions. First, it draws attention to the inevitable relationship between experience and opinion or belief — a relationship which exists even if the person involved is unaware of it. Second, it reminds us of the author, who is creating in this case an association (between experience and idea) which is beyond the grasp of the character. But it reminds us of him obliquely — Joyce is not especially intrusive in the *Portrait*, perhaps because we can easily imagine Stephen as the author, an impression which is modified only by these sly ironies which seem beyond Stephen's power. The reminder amounts to an indication that Joyce may share parts of Stephen's aesthetic, which is presented favourably enough, but that he also goes beyond it by perceiving in it implications of which Stephen is unaware. In particular, we detect Joyce's own conviction that artistic precepts — and hence practice — cannot be divorced from experience. In Stephen he shows how experience generates ideas, then goes on to demonstrate the richer view of art which results when this connection with experience is acknowledged. Stanislaus has commended Joyce's maturity (which by implication can be contrasted with Stephen's relative immaturity in the *Portrait*) by stressing that 'with him there was no scission between life and thought' (*MBK* 163). Stanislaus' conception of maturity here is close to Joyce's own and Stephen is judged in its terms.

Joyce's ironic treatment of Stephen goes further, however, and helps to determine the tone of the novel which is more wry and more comic than solemn critical discussions of it usually manage to imply. For example, when Stephen's lecture on aesthetics is rudely interrupted by a noisy cartload of old iron, 'irony' seems to take physical form as the world of contingency and clutter mocks Stephen's ethereal theorising. Edmund Epstein points out this case, but overlooks another similar instance which might convince sceptical readers that Joyce really does work in this way.[5] During the scene in *Stephen Hero* where Stephen reads his essay on aesthetics to his mother, she is *ironing*. That is, she is enacting an everyday reality which Stephen's earnest pronouncements fail to take into account and which therefore qualifies them.

Stephen's aesthetic is further qualified by the wry disinclination of the *Portrait* — and of Joyce's other works — to accept all its terms. While it may be unreasonable to apply Stephen's definitions rigidly to Joyce's writing and while it is unclear to what extent Stephen believes his lyric-epic-dramatic paradigm applies within a single text, we can hardly help noticing the contrast between an example cited by Stephen, 'that old English ballad *Turpin Hero* which begins

in the first person and ends in the third person' (*P* 215)
and the *Portrait* itself which begins in the third person and
ends in the first. It is striking that all Joyce's works end on an
intensely lyrical and personal note.

Joyce also shows that Stephen takes his various aspirations
a little too seriously, even while the aspirations themselves
are mostly endorsed. Stephen takes wing at the end of each
chapter in the *Portrait* only to be deposited in the world of
squalid appetency at the beginning of the next and this
pattern of ironic deflation is obviously imposed on him by
Joyce as a comment on his premature feelings of exultation.
Although the *Portrait* is as open-ended as possible, Stephen's
final flight will ultimately lead him not to freedom but to
the confines of the Martello Tower with boorish Buck
Mulligan at the beginning of *Ulysses*. Joyce may even have
had an ironic aim in choosing the date for Stephen's first
diary entry, 20 March: it is both Ibsen's birthday and the
beginning of spring, apt congruities which presumably did
not influence Stephen's choice of date.

All these ironies, mild as they are, remind us again that
Stephen is not Joyce and that there is a comic dimension
to the *Portrait*, all the stronger because Stephen is unaware
of it. Stephen's life resembles Joyce's but he is displaced,
living in a different and more sombre environment. He is less
happy, more troubled, than Joyce; he is surrounded by
people less substantial than Joyce's associates were and
consequently seems less intellectually agile and more isolated.
The world mocks his attempts to attain maturity and
individuality. Joyce presents Stephen's ideas seriously enough
but undercuts them by showing their limitations, questioning
whether Stephen understands their full meaning and partly
avoiding them while writing the novel in which they appear.

Ellmann has discussed how Joyce 'mothers' himself in the
Portrait (*JJ* 299). He does not precisely do that. He mothers
a creature close enough to himself to be a family member
but different enough to be his own creation. The detachment
is as necessary to him as the affinity.[6]

It may seem that Joyce has treated Stephen harshly and
he implied a similar judgment himself when he spoke to
Frank Budgen about *Ulysses*: 'I haven't let this young man

off very lightly, have I? Many writers have written about
themselves. I wonder if any one of them has been as candid
as I have?'[7] By 'candid', rather than claiming complete
honesty, Joyce probably meant that his strategy had not
required him to treat Stephen in a favourable light. The
claim is a little disingenuous, since author and character are
sufficiently different to allow Joyce to undermine Stephen
without injury to himself. Yet in some ways Joyce smooths
Stephen's path. After all, he had himself already undergone
the experiences on which Stephen's life was to be approximately based. The kind of anxiety which afflicts most sensitive
people as they confront future choices need play no part in
Stephen's life, since the choices are already made for him.
As early as the opening of the second chapter Stephen feels
a sense of destiny which will involve an important role for
him and perhaps a literary vocation:

> Words which he did not understand he said over and over
> to himself till he had learned them by heart: and through
> them he had glimpses of the real world about him. The
> hour when he too would take part in the life of that world
> seemed drawing near and in secret he began to make ready
> for the great part which he felt awaited him the nature of
> which he only dimly apprehended (*P* 62).

Joyce can plant and develop suggestions in Stephen's life in
the novel earlier than such thoughts may have occurred to
him in reality. Stephen need make no more false turnings
than Joyce feels to be necessary for the purposes of the
novel. Joyce's pretext of studying medicine on his first trip
to Europe, for example, plays no part in the *Portrait*, though
there are hints of it in *Ulysses* and it may even be mocked
obliquely in a conversation between two medical students
(*P* 216). This omission allows Stephen to be a purer artist
than Joyce as he departs for exile. His exile seems more
decisive than Joyce's, which was heavily qualified; as Ellmann
remarks, Joyce 'was neither bidden to leave nor forbidden
to return' (*JJ* 109) and he was in fact to return from his first
hejira after only three weeks. We do not see Stephen's actual
departure, only the preparations for it and the novel ends
with a burst of eloquence which might anticipate a glorious

future in exile for Stephen. *Ulysses*, of course, will show Stephen's attempt at exile to be in some respects a failure. Moreover, if the *Portrait* ends in April of 1903, as Kenner has argued, Stephen will be summoned back to Ireland because of his mother's impending death after only a few weeks. Nevertheless what we see of Stephen at this stage in his career is actually more positive than what we would have seen of Joyce.

Since Stephen's path is smoothed for him, then — because Joyce had already traversed it or one like it — he has no real need to make decisions. Choice and volition are elusive in Joyce's works. He must have made decisions at times but it is possible for even an autobiographical character to evade choice. Stephen, like Bloom after him, seems to have many of his decisions made for him by circumstances, to react rather than to act. His first apparent choice is shown in his complaint to the rector about his unjust punishment at Clongowes, but this is presented as an involuntary action: 'He had reached the door and, turning quickly up to the right, walked up the stairs and, before he could make up his mind to come back, he had entered the low dark narrow corridor that led to the castle' (*P* 55). In this scene, as in the scene with the prostitute which ends the next chapter, Stephen is maturing and changing his state, but in a largely involuntary manner. Such involuntary responses suggest that Stephen is being guided in a particular direction.

Thus the relationship between Joyce and Stephen in the *Portrait* is considerably more intricate than the relationships between the author and the characters in *Dubliners* and it becomes at times the novel's central, if unstated, preoccupation. The *Portrait*, with its austerity, might seem arid if it were not for the exploration of this quirky author-character bond. Moreover, Joyce's relationship with Stephen was something he had to explore and to analyse extensively — as he does in the *Portrait* — before he could create the fascinating characters who appear in his later works and who depend for much of their meaning on the ways in which Joyce bases them on himself.

4

Exiles

Exiles is a problem play. It is, in the first place, unique: no other play by Joyce survives, though there was a much earlier one, *A Brilliant Career*, which he destroyed.[1] The title of this early attempt seems an ironic anticipation of the treatment of Richard Rowan's career in *Exiles*. *Exiles* has also seemed a difficult text to many readers and critics and there have been frequent disputes about its importance and meaning. Before looking at characterisation in *Exiles* it will be helpful to discover why Joyce wrote a play at all and then why he wrote this kind of play in particular.

Drama was one of Joyce's early passions, one which was fostered by his enthusiasm for Ibsen and Hauptmann. In January 1900, as if furnishing a manifesto for the new century, Joyce read his paper 'Drama and Life' to the University College Literary and Historical Society. In this paper he distinguishes 'drama' from mere 'literature'. Drama, he says, 'has to do with the underlying laws first, in all their nakedness and divine severity, and only secondarily with the motley agents who bear them out' (*CW* 40). Drama is

> the interplay of passions to portray truth; drama is strife, evolution, movement in whatever way unfolded; it exists, before it takes form, independently; it is conditioned but not controlled by its scene. . . . However subdued the tone of passions may be, however ordered the action or commonplace the diction, if a play or a work of music or a picture presents the everlasting hopes, desires and hates of us, or deals with a symbolic presentment of our widely related nature . . . then it is drama (*CW* 41).

Joyce's early views of drama can be seen more fully (but

equally fulsomely) in his essay 'Ibsen's New Drama', written at about the same time as 'Drama and Life'. He praises Ibsen's *When We Dead Awaken* for presenting 'countless, indefinable complexities' (*CW* 49); he notes that 'the leaven of prospective drama is gradually discerned working amid the *fin-de-siècle* scene' (*CW* 50), as if dramatic tensions in a play were heightened by an apparently unpropitious setting. He observes that the play proceeds by presenting confessions and notes that Maja and Ulfheim 'are playing as a cat and a bird play' (*CW* 60). Joyce also praises Ibsen, in an essay on *Catilina*, for presenting 'his fable in terms of his characters' (*CW* 100).

It could not be taken for granted — or even expected — that a view of drama reflected in Joyce's early essays, written when he was about eighteen, would influence him when he came to write his own mature play nearly fourteen years later, after he had already found a voice as a short-story writer and novelist. Yet there are striking affinities between the sense of drama delineated in the essays and that present in *Exiles* itself. *Exiles* concerns, very precisely, the 'interplay of passions', though their tone be 'subdued'. The same 'indefinable complexities' which Joyce found in Ibsen also colour *Exiles* and again there is an apparent contradiction between mundane setting and metaphysical action, a contradiction which sets up tensions like those in Ibsen's work. *Exiles* is full of confessions, as Robert Hand observes (*E* 106). Joyce's image for the action involving Maja and Ulfheim ('playing as a cat and a bird play') anticipates his own description of *Exiles* as 'three cat and mouse acts' (*E* 156). *Exiles* also shows Joyce presenting 'his fable in terms of his characters'. Thus while we are not obliged to inspect the early essays to find Joyce's view of drama, it does seem that in writing his play he was still remarkably attuned to his own earlier beliefs. He may have wanted to write a play partly in order to give form to his keen sense of the possibilities of drama.

But this riddle can be asked in another way. If Joyce wrote a play because he had thought extensively about the possibilities of drama, he would also be aware of the need to use material appropriate to the stage. What is it about the theatre which suits the particular concerns of *Exiles* and may help explain why he cast these experiences rather than other ones in dramatic form?

There is a connection between the position of *Exiles* as Joyce's only attempt in its genre and the nature of drama itself. Theatre separates the material in the play from that which is not itself more starkly than novels and stories do. There is no blurred margin, no line where the play shades gradually into the world outside. This characteristic of drama suits Joyce's rigorous exploration, within the play, of a particular, confined situation. The theatrical setting heightens our sense that the solutions to any problems the play presents should be sought, in the first place, within the terms of the problems themselves, not by an appeal to some broader social context, as may be possible in a novel.

Drama also suits Joyce's dislike of explanations, a dislike which marks most of his work. Few prose writers can have avoided exposition as rigorously as Joyce. He tends to be least impressive when he fails to avoid it (as occasionally in *Stephen Hero* and in the opening pages of both 'After the Race' and 'A Painful Case') and to be at his funniest when parodying it (as in the opening pages of the 'Nausicaa' chapter of *Ulysses*). Such reticence is especially appropriate in *Exiles*. In this play the attempt to convey information through speech and gesture is not only a technical pre-occupation but almost a thematic one: the characters themselves explore the possibility of embodying their meanings directly, without explanations. This strategy is evoked light-heartedly in Robert's account of the messages conveyed by various kinds of statues. Exploration of this mode of discourse would be difficult or impossible in a prose text possessing narrative continuity. In a play, where the characters must take full responsibility for conveying meanings, it works well.

Moreover, since within the play on stage there are only speeches and a few actions and within the play as a reading text only speeches and stage directions, there is a feeling of discontinuity by comparison with a piece of narrative prose. Differences between characters tend to be heightened in drama. In Joyce's other works more intrusive narrative methods establish elaborate connections among the characters, so that two people as dissimilar as Leopold Bloom and

Gerty MacDowell can seem, temporarily, to share a similar
state of mind (it is difficult to imagine Bloom and Gerty
onstage together!). In *Exiles*, the characters' speeches appear
pure and stark, vehicles for an interaction which seems to be
limited only by their own wishes and personalities. Even
Robert Hand's pretentious language and demeanour, which
Joyce might have qualified obliquely or even ridiculed in
another work, compete on equal terms with apparently
more admirable forms of address. This quality is particularly
noticeable because in most of the play's scenes only two
characters are present so that an opposition between two
points of view is readily established.

Joyce may have had mixed feelings about exploiting these
aspects of theatre, however well they suited his aims. His
careful preservation of his 'Notes' to *Exiles*, a curious mixture
of plans for sections yet to be written and retrospective
comments on completed sections of the text, seems a belated
attempt to influence interpretations in ways which are more
readily achieved in prose. Joyce refers in these Notes to the
recent 'publication of the lost pages of *Madame Bovary*'
(*E* 150) in which 'the centre of sympathy appears to have
been esthetically shifted from the lover or fancyman to the
husband or cuckold' (a shift which, incidentally, has interesting parallels in both *Exiles* and *Ulysses*). These Notes themselves, published rather like 'lost pages' in 1951, long after the
play's first appearance, might seem an attempt to achieve
similar displacements in his readers' responses to his text,
not that we can be certain Joyce anticipated their publication.
Within the play itself, Joyce seeks to present his fable in
terms of his characters with a minimum of explicit authorial
intervention. Mysterious tensions among the characters can
therefore be sustained with no need for the play to elucidate
them.

By contrast with prose texts, a play puts greater emphasis
on individual characters. We are not distracted from them
by narrative, only passingly by setting and only obliquely
by image and symbol even in a play by Joyce. This emphasis
is particularly marked in a play like *Exiles* where the characters, being aloof from society, have considerable freedom
to choose their own actions and where so much of the

'action' is, in any case, psychological. Admittedly, the two
men in the play are much given to striking a rhetorical pose:
they would, we feel, communicate in earnest soliloquies
and diatribes whether they were in a play or not. This aspect
of them nevertheless increases the appropriateness of the
dramatic form. Since so much emphasis does fall on the
characters in *Exiles*, attention to their creation is vital.

Critics embarking on biographical criticism of Joyce the
playwright might take warning from Stephen Dedalus'
suspect biographical criticism of Shakespeare in the 'Scylla
and Charybdis' episode of *Ulysses*. But that attempt goes
astray less because biographical criticism is inherently mis-
guided than because Stephen lacks the precise information
he would need to make such an analysis valid: these facts
simply do not exist in sufficient quantity in Shakespeare's
case and Stephen's argument is therefore too speculative to
claim literal accuracy, however useful it may be as a parable.
In Joyce's case the facts usually do exist — indeed he often
took pains to preserve them — and we might therefore take
Stephen's Shakespeare discussion as an oblique invitation
to perform such an analysis of *Exiles*. Stephen's comments
on Shakespeare imply that in *Ulysses* he no longer believes
what he claimed to believe in the *Portrait*, that in drama
the writer should 'disappear'. It may be relevant to his
changed opinion that *Exiles* was written after the *Portrait*
and before 'Scylla and Charybdis' and *Exiles* is a play in
which the writer, while discreet, is not as far from the action
as Stephen in the *Portrait* implied he should be.

Exiles prompts us to make the kind of author-character
association already made for *Dubliners*. Richard Rowan's
name, for example, alliterates like James Joyce's. He is a
creative writer (apparently a novelist) who puts his friends
into his books. He lives with an uneducated woman and
a young son. He is proud, solitary, easily moved to jealousy
and suspicion; he fears but also courts betrayal. He feels
alienated from Ireland, having spent several years on the
Continent but also feels a bond with his homeland and
returns to face the consequences of his exile. It is 1912, the
year of Joyce's last visit to Ireland.

One of the play's central problems may be simplified by

recognising the detailed ways in which Richard is based on Joyce. This problem is Richard's heroism. Bertha seems to accept this heroism as a reality and it is hard to read the play logically if we deny it. Yet Richard has some unappealing qualities, including masochism, a touch of paranoia, aloofness and a tendency to manipulate people (despite his own defence of freedom and doubt). These attributes are readily observed in Joyce also and therefore the presentation of Richard strikes us as impressively candid. Such candour closely resembles Richard's own desired intellectual stance, contributing to the complex affinity between author and character. Richard's heroism is substantiated by our sense that Joyce acknowledges openly the faults he and Richard share.

There is a further affinity. Richard wishes to manipulate the other characters as if he were a playwright himself. He uses them to act out his own drama just as Joyce uses all the characters, but especially Richard, to act out a drama based largely on his own life. Richard's isolation and suffering are partly a drama played out for his own benefit, as was Joyce's exile. Richard's histrionic habits – he beats rhetorically on doors which would easily open if he turned the handle – may acknowledge similar failings in Joyce.

Richard also borrows a few characteristics from John Joyce which, given Joyce's attitudes to his father, do not necessarily drive a wedge between author and character but may rather enrich Joyce's presentation of himself. In particular, Richard's relationships with his parents and especially his final leavetakings from them before their deaths, are based on John Joyce's experience. Richard's two farewells are so neatly counterpointed that it is remarkable to find both had an authentic source and a shared one at that (this is not the only case where the world seems to have been arranged for Joyce's convenience). In the cases of both Richard Rowan and John Joyce the mother objected to the son's choice of a mate and hardened her heart against him, dying without seeking a reconciliation (Gabriel Conroy also owes something to this episode). The father, in striking contrast, urged the son not to remain at his deathbed but to go and hear an opera instead. Although these incidents come from the life of Joyce's father they are used as occasions for meditations on Joyce's feelings about his own parents.

Richard Rowan's name has some outward-looking implications as well. It links him with Archibald Hamilton Rowan the Irish rebel hero and though Richard denies descent from this man he seems to have named his son Archie after him. The rowan tree, as has been pointed out before, is the ash, source of the ashplant walking-stick which Stephen Dedalus carries in *Ulysses* as the mark of a poet. The rowan tree is also reputed to ward off evil spirits and Richard has some of these to contend with and exorcise, as he says explicitly in Act III. The word 'rich' which his name evokes has historically implied power as well as wealth and Robert makes much of Richard's 'strength'. 'Richard' means literally 'rule hard' and so is an appropriate name for someone of Richard's rigorous and demanding disposition.

Robert Hand is a perplexing character because he seems so changeable and various. This quality may show his rather diabolical wiliness but it also owes something to the fact that he is a composite figure built up from a series of antagonists to Joyce, as well as incorporating some of Joyce's own attributes – just as Robert is both an antagonist to Richard and a reduced version of him.

Robert seems to acquire from Oliver Gogarty his appearance, some mannerisms, aspects of his mercurial nature and an apparent tendency to be rebellious and emotionally aggressive but actually conservative and intellectually cowardly. Gogarty was Joyce's principal opponent and the source of Buck Mulligan in *Ulysses* (the first chapter of which, where Mulligan is most oppressively dominant, Joyce was writing at about the same time as *Exiles*). Thomas Kettle has been identified as the source of Robert's attempt to arrange an academic position for Richard and his writing of a newspaper article about his repatriated friend. Not especially sinister in themselves, these two actions in the play nevertheless seem an attempt by Robert to gain power over Richard, to keep him in Dublin and to hold over his head the threats of the establishment and public opinion, dragging the independent Richard down to Robert's level of social acquiescence. Finally, two men who claimed or sought romantic connections with Nora, Vincent Cosgrave and Roberto Prezioso, are generally accepted as sources for Robert Hand as would-be (if half-hearted) seducer.[2] Joyce exploited the Cosgrave and Prezioso connections for his own purposes in actuality and in the play Robert's attempt to win over Bertha seems another way of gaining power over Richard; Robert's main aim may not be to seduce the wife but to reduce the husband.

The importance of these models in the play is considerable. They help to show why Robert is treated with apparent seriousness despite his occasionally ridiculous behaviour. Gogarty/Mulligan, for example, could also be ridiculous but was no less dangerous for that; indeed, in his antics he sometimes used the artist's weapons against the artist himself, as Robert does with Richard.

Robert's materialism, pragmatism and easy sensuality contrast strikingly with Richard's qualities. Yet Robert also appears as a Richard-like being who has failed to mature. He still speaks what Richard calls 'the language of my youth' (*E* 89), lives in the manner Richard had once made his own and visits the cottage Richard had once shared with him. Robert remains a bachelor and (at least in his own estimation) a playboy, while Richard has, in his own terms, taken on family responsibilities. Robert also has something of the courtly lover about him, while Richard expresses more 'modern' views of love. There is a connection here with 'The Dead': in his courtly aspect Robert recalls Gabriel Conroy and his image of Bertha as 'something beautiful and distant — the moon or some deep music' (*E* 35) recalls the business about 'distant music' in the story. Also like Gabriel, Robert appears poised between crassness and idealism — between, we might say, the possibilities embodied in Freddy Malins and in Michael Furey, two characters who are contrasted but who share their initials and (with Robert Hand as well as with one another) the epithet 'poor fellow'. Robert shares Freddy's tendency to nervous banter and Michael's tendency to stand in the rain outside the house where his beloved is present; Gabriel seems similarly poised between these alternatives, as he shows in his chastened self-image as a 'pitiable fatuous fellow' (*D* 220) and his attempted identification with Michael Furey. Richard has risen, or attempted to rise, above both alternatives.

Yet there are frequent reminders of the similarities between Richard and Robert even as we see that Richard has risen to a higher level. One of the simplest but most striking indications of their affinity is provided by their identical postures in their respective first appearances in the play, approaching Beatrice with a hand outstretched in greeting. Robert produces newspaper articles while Richard produces imaginative literature; but both are writers and both write about their friends.

Just as Robert resembles Richard and differs from him, so he embodies aspects of Joyce as well as of his opponents. Joyce had written for newspapers on several occasions, if more intelligently than Robert does (Leopold Bloom will also be associated with a newspaper). Joyce, more specifically, wrote for Italian newspapers, which Richard continues to receive after his return to Ireland. Joyce, like Robert, at times played the sentimentalist or courtly lover, as in his prose poem *Giacomo Joyce*, a source for some of the imagery and moods of *Exiles*. Robert sounds like Joyce in letters to Nora when Bertha becomes for him 'a wild flower blowing in a hedge' (*E* 35). But it is Richard who more accurately embodies Joyce's later attitudes to relationships: to Bertha he expresses his wish 'to hold you by no bonds, even of love, to be united with you in body and soul in utter nakedness' (*E* 147).

Robert Hand's first name links him with Roberto Prezioso, but the play also intends a pun on 'robber': Robert is seen as the 'thief' who would steal from the rich Richard his treasure, Bertha. Robert's surname Hand conveys his manipulative nature, his affinity with the body rather than the mind, and may also link him, as Sheldon Brivic has suggested, with Hand the leader of the fallen sons of Albion in Blake's *Jerusalem*, who like Robert is associated with stone, inanimate matter, particular dwelling places (Ranelagh, Surrey) and hypocrisy.[3] (*Exiles* may owe more to Blake; Richard's moral scheme seems to have affinities with *The Marriage of Heaven and Hell*, for example. Joyce had given lectures on Blake in 1912.)

Bertha is the most attractive major character in the play, a kind of Molly Bloom without the harshness Molly sometimes displays. Molly's pragmatic evaluations of Bloom and Boylan contrast with Bertha's generosity towards both Robert and Richard, two men who will strike many readers and audiences as unworthy of her. The play confirms that Bertha has a strong instinctive understanding of the emotional complexities of the two men and that she understands them without needing the posturing and statements of policy which they themselves seem to require before reacting to anything.

Bertha's debt to Nora is obvious and confirmed by Joyce in the Notes. Bertha nevertheless seems gentler and more sympathetic than the public Nora and may depict a more domestic side of her, one which had also appeared in the presentation of Gretta Conroy. Like Nora, Bertha has coped with the problems of exile and of living with a man of difficult temperament and seems to have been strengthened by such trials. By heightening some of his own weaknesses in the treatment of Richard and showing Bertha responding with few complaints, Joyce may be paying tribute to Nora's fortitude.

Bertha's name suggests 'birth' and 'earth' by sound and 'bright' by etymology; in the play she is associated with motherhood, the earth and the moon. She is also associated with water (she has just been swimming when the play begins) and specifically with the rain in Act II. When she arrives at the cottage she carries no protection against the rain, while Richard carries an umbrella. The rain is fertile; Robert speaks of 'summer rain on the earth. . . . The darkness and warmth and flood of passion' (*E* 113). Bertha is thus associated with nature and in particular with water in its positive aspects.

Of the main characters, Beatrice Justice is at once the least complex in terms of personality and the most puzzling in terms of the play. She is a cousin of Robert's and was once engaged to him; this engagement contrasts with the decision of Richard and Bertha to live together unmarried and so suggests the more conventional nature of both Robert and Beatrice. Beatrice has been a friend of Richard's and he has written about her, but most of whatever affection this relationship contained appears to have been on her side. She has been seen by some critics as an intellectual; she does have a disembodied and aloof quality, wears glasses and gives music lessons, but she is hardly intelligent — her enthusiastic reaction to Robert's chilly article about Richard demonstrates her obtuseness.

Joyce acknowledges that Beatrice's role in the play is problematic. One of the Notes observes that 'during the second act as Beatrice is not on the stage, her figure must appear before the audience through the thoughts or speech of the others. This is by no means easy' (*E* 159). It is by no means easy partly because the other characters all have their own preoccupations and difficulties during this time and have little apparent reason to think of Beatrice.

Just as Robert's complex and even erratic personality can be linked with his multiple sources, so Beatrice's ethereal personality can be associated with the tenuousness of her sources. It has been suggested that Beatrice is modelled on Amalia Popper, the girl supposedly depicted in *Giacomo Joyce* and there are verbal and imagistic resemblances in the presentation of the two characters. But Amalia when Joyce knew her was adolescent, lively, apparently flirtatious and the object of a brief infatuation on Joyce's part, whereas Beatrice is older, jaded and seemingly frigid and treated by Richard with harshness and even hostility. If Joyce did have himself and Amalia in mind here, he has reversed their roles, as with Frank and Eveline if he was thinking of himself and Nora, though neither of these hypotheses is convincing. It is difficult to imagine Joyce taking much interest in a person like Beatrice, at least after he met Nora. Beatrice seems closer to the middle-class girls Joyce had known in Dublin, or to E—C— in the *Portrait*, whom Stephen leaves because she is too conventional to share in the life of an artist.

If Beatrice fails to come to life in the play, it may be because she failed to come to life in life, or as a part of Joyce's imagination. She is all too clearly a possibility which must be rejected. The character-contrasts she makes possible do, however, establish a case for the kind of spontaneity of behaviour which Joyce displayed and admired throughout his life. Beatrice's frigidity and Robert's musty sentimentality, represented by his overblown roses and his perfumed, velvet-jacketed over-preparation for Bertha's visit, contrast with Bertha's instinctive nature and Richard's attempts at intellectual freedom.

Beatrice Justice's first name, ironically in terms of the play, means 'making happy'. The echo of Dante is also ironical: this Beatrice is a flawed figure of inspiration. The quality of 'justice' contrasts with the mercy or generosity displayed by the warmer, more instinctive Bertha. In the Notes Joyce describes Beatrice as cold and it is worth observing that both her names incorporate the word 'ice'; if Bertha represents water in its positive aspects, Beatrice Justice, we might say with slight exaggeration, is 'just ice'.

Thus an inspection of sources for the characters in *Exiles* does overcome some of the play's problems, especially those posed by Richard's heroism, Joyce's attitude to Robert and Beatrice's role in the play. The least problematic character, Bertha, has a single living source; the character who seems least at home in the play, Beatrice, apparently has no close source in reality. The puzzles posed by the men bear some relation to the nature of their origins.

The significance of *Exiles* cannot be fully understood unless these facts are taken into account. The complexity and the discomforts of the play are deeply personal, in all senses of the word. For example, Richard's wish to impose on Bertha a freedom which she does not seek arises partly from masochism, partly from a stern intellectual logic and partly from his compassion for her and his fear that he might accept loyalty from her and so make her life poorer in love. Without tracing these forces back to Joyce's life it is more difficult to account adequately for the play's peculiar, brooding intensity, occasional morbidity, final sense of heavily qualified victory, or the cryptic, shorthand manner in which complex emotional states are occasionally treated. Though the dramatic form insists that solutions to the play's problems must be sought first within the terms of the play, Joyce never completely cut the link between the play and himself. Confirmation for this continued link can be found in his correspondence which follows his solicitous guidance of *Exiles* through its various translations and performances.

The sources of discomfort and suffering which are treated in *Exiles* are common to many people, but they are treated through circumstances particularly close to those of Joyce's life. The play touches on the possible difficulties of relationships with sexual partners, friends, and parents, on the sense of entrapment which any relationship may impose and on the guilt which may arise from reflection about one's effects on another person's life. Richard acquires Joyce's kinds of guilt and his strategies for dealing with guilt. The decisions he must make are difficult ones which may hurt, as much as help, the person who makes them, but they must be made: nobody will prefer Robert who escapes such decisions, to Richard, who has to make them. The play defends Joyce's view of relationships, an attitude which insists on taking into account the paradoxes and inconsistencies which are part of the self. Joyce aggressively probes ideals of eternal fidelity and filial acquiescence, showing the pain but also the strength which, he argues, result from an admission of the limitations of human feeling and endeavour.

Exiles was written after the *Portrait* and before the bulk of *Ulysses*; in fact, Joyce stopped work on *Ulysses* for a time in order to complete the play first. *Exiles* does function as a transitional stage in the pattern of Joyce's works, especially in terms of characterisation.

Exiles anticipates both *Ulysses* and *Finnegans Wake* in being set wholly in Dublin and covering a period of about eighteen hours. Like *Ulysses,* it opens on a warm day in June. *Exiles* ends with Richard exhausted and apparently falling asleep while Bertha continues to reflect on their relationship, her thoughts culminating in an affirmation of love for him. This scene closely anticipates the ending of *Ulysses* and also resembles the final scene of the *Wake*. Richard Rowan's name associates him with a tree, while Robert is repeatedly associated with stones. The antagonists in *Finnegans Wake*, Shem and Shaun, will also be associated with tree and stone respectively.

Exiles might seem to anticipate the 'Circe' chapter of *Ulysses* which is set out as if it were a play. 'Circe', like *Exiles*, is a psychological test and analysis of its central characters. Nevertheless, there is a considerable difference between a play seriously intended for stage performance and a 'dramatic' episode in a novel, especially one like 'Circe' which pointedly blurs the distinction between what actually takes place (those events whose reality is confirmed by the more determinate naturalism of adjacent and later episodes) and what takes place only in the characters' minds (or, more accurately, in the mind of the reader). 'Circe' would also be difficult to stage because so much of its material is by conventional standards highly improper; in casting this material in theatrical form Joyce may be punning on the notion that it is the most 'obscene' — the furthest from potential stage representation — of any episode in *Ulysses*.

Yet a common feature which does unite *Exiles* and 'Circe' is their scepticism about facts. In both cases, the seemingly objective dramatic form guarantees not certainty about what is really going on, but rather doubt, partly because we are confined to those scenes represented to us and cannot tell what is happening 'offstage'. Richard says 'I can never know, never in this world. I do not wish to know or to believe' (*E* 147). Joyce himself remarked to a friend that 'life is suspended in doubt like the world in the void. You might find this in some sense treated in *Exiles*' (*JJ* 557). 'Circe' only expresses more acutely a concern with uncertainty which is found throughout *Ulysses* and in the *Portrait* as well.

In both novels, it is suggested that love between mother and child may be the only certainty. Cranly affirms that 'whatever else is unsure in this stinking dunghill of a world a mother's love is not' (*P* 241–2). At this stage Stephen rightly construes Cranly's comments as an attempt to make him conform but in *Ulysses*, after his own mother has died, Stephen reflects that '*amor matris*, subjective and objective genitive, may be the only true thing in life' (*U* 207). This possibility seems muted in *Exiles* and Richard expresses great bitterness towards his mother, as if intent on destroying even this last tenuous 'certainty'. Yet in the relationship of young Archie to his parents, particularly to Bertha, much of the elusive warmth of *Exiles* is concentrated. Archie seems the most unequivocally positive character in the play and his relationship with Bertha the least complex, least tortured and most promising. Joyce remarks in one of the Notes that 'the love of Bertha for her child must be brought out as strongly and as simply and as early as possible in the third act' (*E* 159). In *Ulysses* too, parenthood is the nearest Joyce can offer to an ideal.

But doubt remains pervasive and it is symbolised for Joyce, in *Exiles* and elsewhere, by the idea of infidelity, which shows that we cannot know definitively even those people to whom we feel closest. *Exiles* is Joyce's first extended treatment of a marital relationship, something which becomes a central concern in *Ulysses*. The relationship portrayed in *Exiles* faces problems which will recur in *Ulysses*. Both Richard and Bloom have avoided sleeping with their wives, for an indefinite period in Richard's case and for over ten years in Bloom's. In both works the marital relationship is threatened — but also brought to a focus — by a male rival, unsuccessful in *Exiles*, successful (in a limited sense) in *Ulysses* and in both cases the rival evokes in the husband a complex reaction in which there is more acquiescence than indignation, though Richard seems more excited and less distressed than Bloom about the possibility of being cuckolded.

As a treatment of marital relationships, *Exiles* suggests two lines of development which Joyce may well have contemplated for *Ulysses* and then abandoned. First, in *Exiles* he enters the mind of the would-be lover as well as of the husband; whereas in *Ulysses*, while deeply involved with Bloom's consciousness, he never shows Boylan from within (with the sole exception of Boylan's stream-of-consciousness fragment 'A young pullet' [*U* 228]; this only reinforces our sense that Boylan is presented mostly in terms of externals, just as he sees others in the same way). Second, in *Exiles* the artist-figure is presented in the role of the husband, something Joyce never attempted again: Stephen in *Ulysses* is remote from valuable relationships while Richard, for all his problems, does have Bertha. It is possible that the writing of *Exiles* diverted Joyce from these approaches, so reinforcing the basic patterns of *Ulysses*: solitary artist, cuckolded husband viewed from within, shallow lover seen from out-

side. Bertha from *Exiles* can become Molly Bloom by the
addition of tinges of vulgarity and defiance; Beatrice, whose
role was always tenuous, disappears.

Richard's compassion for Bertha (he fears to make her
life poorer in love) has affinities with Bloom's attitude to
Molly. Apart from masochism, Bloom's partial acceptance
of Molly's affair with Boylan shows his sensitivity to her
fears of aging, of neglect. He does not blame her for seeking
elsewhere what he has failed to provide.

Exiles also marks a transitional stage between the *Portrait*
and *Ulysses* in its treatment of relationships with parents. In
the *Portrait*, Stephen's mother is a shadowy figure who
generally nurtures her son, though Stephen's ominous dispute
with her about religion is mentioned late in the novel. In
Ulysses she becomes, after her death, a chastising figure who
evokes Stephen's guilt throughout the book. Richard's
relationship with his mother, though borrowed in part from
John Joyce's life, heralds this transition; Richard says bitterly
that his mother 'died alone, not having forgiven me and
fortified by the rites of holy church' (*E* 23). In the *Portrait*
Stephen's father often seems a burden to him while in
Ulysses there is greater detachment between them; Simon
Dedalus still behaves irresponsibly towards his children but
we also see him as a *bon vivant*. Again, Richard's relationship
with his father, his 'smiling handsome father' (*E* 25),
anticipates this change.

Exiles was Joyce's first work to be completed after the
formulation of Stephen's pronouncements on drama in the
Portrait. Just as the *Portrait* itself seemed to qualify the
value of Stephen's views, so too does *Exiles*. For Joyce does
not fully achieve the impersonal state Stephen associates
with drama. He projects himself into the characters in *Exiles*
as strenuously as he does in his other works. This method
gives *Exiles* a somewhat novelistic tone. Joyce may have
assumed that his choice of the dramatic mode would in itself
guarantee that no personal elements should be obtrusive.
Yet the personal elements still impose themselves on our
attention, because they so often seem necessary to explain
quirks in the play. Some of the difficulty of *Exiles* arises
from the paradox that Joyce had personal things to say and

deliberately chose a supposedly impersonal medium in which to say them.

This paradox may, finally, help to explain why Joyce abandoned drama after a single mature play. Just as each experimental episode of *Ulysses* was to leave behind it a burnt-up field which Joyce would not seek to recultivate, just as *Dubliners* had exploited the ability of short stories to express stasis and discontinuity, so *Exiles* stretches to the limit the usefulness to Joyce of the dramatic form. Drama suited the starkness, isolation and intensity implicit in the play's themes; to repeat himself in the same genre might have been for Joyce both a dilution and a contradiction in terms.

5

Ulysses

I: *Stephen*

One of many remarkable facts about *Ulysses* is that in it we meet for the first time in works published by Joyce, a major character whom we have already met in an earlier work. Stephen Dedalus appears on the first page of *Ulysses* as he does on the last page of the *Portrait*. What we seem at first to be offered is a sequel to that book, showing Stephen's later fortunes, perhaps his artistic maturity.

This continuity of character is especially striking because of the rigid separation of characters within and between Joyce's earlier works. Even in *Dubliners*, no important character appears in more than one story (unless we take the first three narrators to be the same boy, in a hypothesis which is plausible but for which proof is deliberately withheld by the text). No major *Dubliners* character appears in the *Portrait*; nor does Stephen's family appear in *Dubliners* (Stephen can be compared with the first three *Dubliners* narrators but is not identical with any of them), even though the Dedaluses lived in Dublin at the time the events shown in the stories took place. Kate Morkan, from 'The Dead', is revealed in *Ulysses* to be Stephen's godmother, but this connection is nowhere mentioned or implied in *Dubliners* or the *Portrait* (perhaps Joyce had not even envisaged the relationship when he wrote those books). Characters in *Exiles*, too, appear in no other work. Thus in Joyce's works before *Ulysses* characters are unique, confined to the work which contains them and the works are thereby marked as discrete, treatments of separate areas of reality.

Later in *Ulysses* we will find other characters from the early works. *Dubliners* characters such as Martin Cunningham, Bob Doran and Tom Kernan reappear in their own persons, while Mrs Sinico, Gabriel and Gretta Conroy, Bartell D'Arcy, Julia Morkan and others are mentioned. Characters from the *Portrait* who reappear in *Ulysses* include Lynch, Dante Riordan and Father Conmee.

Stephen's appearance on the first page thus establishes a new pattern in *Ulysses*: this novel may bring together people who have previously been confined to separate works. This change will become vital in determining the kind of reality created in *Ulysses*: more comprehensive, more willing to make comparisons and assimilate contraries, than was the case in the earlier works. Among the diverse entities *Ulysses* is capable of assimilating and fusing are those earlier works themselves.

It should be mentioned here that the relationship between *Ulysses* and Joyce's earlier works owes something to the origins of *Ulysses*: initially conceived as a *Dubliners* story and gradually assimilating material split off from the end of the *Portrait*, it was bound to bridge its predecessors to some degree. Yet this historical accident becomes an active principle as Joyce elaborates the retrospective associations far beyond the inevitable. He fuses the episodic, disjunctive mode of *Dubliners* with the progressive mode of the *Portrait* to create the characteristic dual movement of *Ulysses*.

But is Stephen in fact the 'same' character we know from the *Portrait*?

His distinctive name makes the identification emphatic. The first mention of him has a casual tone which suggests the reappearance of the familiar rather than the appearance of the new; though we must always be careful with Joyce's introductions, since it is typical of him to introduce new characters as if we have known them for years. We find a reference to Cranly (*U* 7), Stephen's friend in the *Portrait* who affected his thoughts towards the end of that novel, particularly in his diary. A few pages later comes a reference to Stephen carrying the boat of incense at Clongowes, another scene familiar to us from the *Portrait*, qualified now by the parallel with Mulligan's mock-mass on the first page of *Ulysses*. These references imply that the Stephen of *Ulysses* has the same past as the character we already know who bears his name.

If this identification of the history of the two Stephens is complete — and nothing in *Ulysses* disproves it — then we know a great deal about him already, even before we meet him in 'Telemachus'. Joyce's insistence that translation of *Ulysses* into a particular language depended on the prior translation of the *Portrait* into that language again reinforces his emphasis on this connection. The information about Stephen's past provided in the *Portrait* must be available to all readers of *Ulysses*. The special relationship most readers of *Ulysses* feel they have with Stephen rests in part on this previous knowledge and it is the sheer attractiveness of the familiar which helps to retain our sympathy for Stephen even as he is shown to possess new unattractive qualities or intensifications of ones he had in the *Portrait* (arrogance leading to a touch of cruelty, for example). If we were not already disposed to like Stephen, we might risk losing sympathy with him at some point in the early episodes.[1]

We deduce from 'Telemachus', then, that Stephen is older by perhaps a year than he was at the end of the *Portrait*, that he is sharing a tower with Buck Mulligan (unmentioned and unheralded in the *Portrait*) and Haines. Haines is also unheralded in the *Portrait* and Stephen has met him recently — perhaps when Haines moved in, three days earlier by the evidence of the tower's suddenly increased milk consumption (*U* 15). Stephen's mother has died since we left him in the *Portrait* and he has refused to pray at her deathbed, a refusal which may make us recall the quarrel with his mother about religion to which he alluded near the end of the *Portrait*. Her death and his response to it fill him with guilt, which he at once heightens and attempts to qualify by attacking Mulligan's insensitivity on the subject. Mulligan's 'damn you and your Paris fads' (*U* 12) hints to us that Stephen has been in Europe, as he intended at the end of the *Portrait*, an impression which will soon be confirmed. Stephen's prompt return to Ireland was not anticipated in the *Portrait*, however; nor was the job we find him to hold currently, that of a teacher.

Taking the Stephen of 'Telemachus' to be simply an older version of the one in the *Portrait*, we find that his plans there have scarcely been fulfilled. Instead of freedom on the Continent he still suffers bondage in Ireland, trapped in the prison-like tower the key to which Mulligan insists on retaining. Having declined to stay with Cranly, he lives with the far more oppressive Mulligan, who is a mock-priest rather than the priest of eternal imagination Stephen aspired to be and who also seeks to usurp Stephen's role as a lord of language: Mulligan has eight speeches before Stephen manages to say anything at all. Stephen must also put up with the insufferable Haines who has frivolously exiled himself in the opposite direction from Stephen's planned, serious flight, bringing his tyrannies and insensitivities with him and offers inane babbling and obtuseness instead of Stephen's 'silence . . . and cunning'. (His name suggests 'hatreds' and he embodies the threatening forces of history and England; Stephen, seeing Haines as a symbol of oppression, complains to him also of the bondage imposed by Ireland and by Catholicism.)

It is as if Stephen has chosen masochistically to live in a setting which dramatises his discontent and his sense of failure. Although Stephen seems physically free of his mother, by her death and of his father, by his own flight from home and deliberate or accidental evasion during the day, parents still weigh heavily on his thoughts. Indeed, 'Telemachus' establishes that Stephen's plans, announced at the end of the *Portrait*, could scarcely have gone more seriously astray than they have. The opening of *Ulysses* undermines retrospectively the ending of the *Portrait*, just as each chapter of that novel undermined its predecessor. Stephen's inertia and desolation in 'Telemachus' are caused partly by his fall back into a world he had tried to escape.

We are bound to wonder why Stephen's plans have gone wrong. To answer this question we need to take up hints which appear later in the novel, including Stephen's fullest recollections of his recent days, in 'Proteus'. He reflects on his time in Paris, where he has studied *'physiques, chimiques et naturelles'* (*U* 41) as if, like Joyce, he was beginning (or playing at beginning) a medical degree. He has been called back from Paris because of his mother's death, her terminal illness coinciding with his abortive study of the art of healing. We find that this death occurred about a year before the date of *Ulysses* – Stephen's mother was buried on 26 June 1903 – and it seems possible that Stephen has been back to Paris more recently, if his fantasy about an alibi needed if he were arrested for murder is to be taken as an authentic recollection. We might suspect this alibi to be a Joycean joke disguising the fact that Stephen was elsewhere (presumably in Dublin) on the date in question, but other evidence helps to locate him in Paris.[2]

If Stephen has indeed returned to Paris recently, this second visit seems to have made him no happier than his earlier one, if only because his second return to Ireland emphasises again and more forcefully, his failure to escape. While we are not told explicitly what has brought him back to Ireland again, the most likely reason (to judge by his present state and by sly glances at Joyce's biography) is poverty – which would mean, chiefly, that his intellectual and spiritual aspirations have yet to free themselves from worldly facts. Stephen's Paris memories display great beauty as well as some pretentiousness (*U* 42–4), but they do not seem a sufficient reward for his efforts.

Thus the Stephen Dedalus we meet early in *Ulysses* is a person we watch attentively and with some sympathy since we feel we know him already. He is a brilliant young man whose aspirations have not been fulfilled and who seeks compensation for his disappointment in aloofness and hostility, who sharply criticises himself and those around him and whose edge of masochism is displayed in his mental self-flagellation over his mother's death and his continued contact with Mulligan, who torments him almost as mercilessly as he torments himself. His sense of dispossession is something he heightens deliberately and in fact there is a moment when he apparently seeks to win us over to his position by deception. When Stephen reflects of the tower key 'It is mine, I paid the rent' (*U* 20) he anticipates and accentuates his sense of grievance at Mulligan's insistence on keeping the key. But it is surprising that the heavily indebted Stephen should have paid the rent and it seems possible either that he is quoting a remark of Mulligan's (as Kenner and others have suggested; if this interpretation is correct, it points to previous arguments between Stephen and Mulligan over the symbolic possession of that key) or that he is simply fibbing, for his own benefit or for ours. In either case his tone here is disgruntled and self-righteous, however obnoxious Mulligan's behaviour may in fact have been.

As we respond to these emotionally complex (if also bleak) impressions, we are likely in the process to neglect Stephen's relationship to Joyce, which seemed central and inescapable in the *Portrait*. The presentation of Stephen in *Ulysses* is so much more subtle and elaborate than it was in the *Portrait* that, at least till Bloom appears, it becomes in itself a sufficient focus for our attention. The *Portrait* continually posed the question of the autobiographical author's relationship to his persona and inevitably we wondered what Joyce thought about this connection. In *Ulysses* the relationship is buried more deeply and we wonder whether it is still a main concern.

If the Stephen of *Ulysses* is indeed identical with the Stephen of the *Portrait*, as he seems to be in terms of his own criterion of memory rather than molecules, he shares many of Joyce's past experiences, as we have already seen. Experiences he has undergone since his *Portrait* days resemble Joyce's as well, most prominently the loss of his mother and his visit to Paris. His Paris experiences, particularly, seem to be based directly on Joyce's own. Some of Stephen's Paris impressions had already been noted by Joyce on his own account: 'Paris rawly waking, crude sunlight on her lemon streets. Moist pith of farls of bread, the froggreen wormwood, her matin incense, court the air. . . . Faces of Paris men go by, . . . wellpleased pleasers, curled conquistadores' (*U* 42). Stephen and Joyce both recorded this response after their visits to Paris. Nevertheless, Joyce's own recorded impressions of Paris are mannered, already literary, already resembling those of a persona (the Observant Slightly Disaffected Young Man in Exile); even if he had not yet envisaged the figure of Stephen Dedalus when he recorded them, we might say that Stephen represents that side of Joyce which the Paris recollections express and who could therefore arise effortlessly to utter them in his own person, or onto whom they could be unobtrusively grafted. It is also true that there is a naïveté about Stephen's Paris memories which Joyce would presumably have excised if he were publishing the material as his own recollections and this naïveté distinguishes author from persona. Yet we cannot rule out the possibility that Stephen, too, is aware of this naïve quality and uses it to tease himself — or us.

Stephen on Bloomsday still resembles the Joyce of June 1904 in many ways, though in a few cases Stephen's situation on Bloomsday is based on Joyce's life at a slightly earlier or later date. They share their quarters in the Martello Tower (though Joyce lived there later in 1904 and perhaps more briefly than Stephen does), a teaching job in Dalkey and the troubling but somehow compelling company of Gogarty/ Mulligan. Some time that summer Joyce was knocked down in the street, as Stephen will be later in the novel, then apparently rescued by a man rather like Bloom.[3]

Yet Joyce and Stephen are also growing apart, even in measurable naturalistic ways. At one end of the spectrum of differences are minute details we will never know because Joyce chose to keep them to himself; at the other are vital and accessible matters. The margin between these areas has that living quality of flux which distinguishes so much of *Ulysses* and which seems designed to frustrate our attempts to separate art from the life in which it is based. This intention, incidentally, explains why attempts to make such distinctions (as undertaken by many critics) often reveal very little. Fastidious attempts to pry all of Joyce's facts loose from his fictions argue for a kind of novel nobody would want to read (and which nobody would worry about not possessing) and may create more problems than they solve. At the same time, such an intention on Joyce's part is not an argument for ignoring biographical evidence altogether; his own alertness to the utility of such evidence obliges us to investigate what he is doing with it.

The most obvious and probably the most important 'vital matter' is that 16 June 1904 marks the beginning of Joyce's relationship with Nora Barnacle, as measured sacramentally by himself. It would be difficult to overestimate the importance of this choice of date and our familiarity with the choice should not hide the remarkable way Joyce found to commemorate his anniversary. This selection of a personally crucial day as the date of *Ulysses* shows, in a way which the novel nowhere needs to make explicit, just how far Joyce has moved from Stephen's position.

Stephen's lack of a relationship resembling Joyce's with Nora is conspicuous and one of the first things Bloom comments on as soon as he can politely do so (while Stephen, ironically, is unconscious; this is also the only moment when Bloom calls Stephen by his first name, as if while Stephen is conscious Bloom is too timid or too tied by the conventions of the day to challenge the young man's aloofness). Moreover, it is extremely difficult to imagine Stephen, as we see him, entering into such a relationship even if the opportunity for it arose (as it could have – Joyce met Nora in the street and Stephen spends plenty of time in the street; though, interestingly, we never see him in Nassau Street where Joyce met Nora).

But even more significantly, it is difficult to imagine Stephen possessing or acquiring a sensibility which could translate a chance meeting into a sacred anniversary and then write a book to commemorate it. Those optimists who believe Stephen goes off at the end of the novel in order to write the novel overlook the fact that in *Ulysses* Stephen is conspicuously denied that relationship which *Ulysses* is partly written to celebrate. There are other serious objections to the theory as well, including further differences between Stephen's personality and Joyce's. Stephen's physical decrepitude, which sets off the brilliance of his mind, is an exaggeration of the health problems of Joyce who looks fit enough in photographs taken in 1904. Conceivably Stephen's brilliance, too, is a heightened version of Joyce's at that date (authors can easily create characters more intelligent than themselves by showing the characters possessing insights at a younger age, or thinking faster, than they themselves did). In any case, Joyce and Stephen are not identical and there is no evidence that Stephen writes *Ulysses*.

If Stephen and Joyce diverge on Bloomsday – if, indeed, *Ulysses* was written partly to document that divergence – it does not follow that Stephen's future will resemble Joyce's.

It has been argued by critics that the places and dates noted at the end of the *Portrait* ('Dublin 1904 Trieste 1914', *P* 253) delineate Stephen's future as well as Joyce's. This interpretation is questionable and nobody has suggested that the parallel entry in *Ulysses* ('Trieste–Zürich–Paris, 1914–1921', *U* 783) relates to the life of Molly, who has just been narrating – but nor does it self-evidently relate to Stephen. Rather, these entries seem to be shorthand depictions of the relationship between Joyce's life and his works and signs of his authority, like the epigraph to the *Portrait* and the title, *Ulysses*. (Joyce became increasingly possessive about such signs; having accepted Stanislaus' suggested titles *Chamber Music, Stephen Hero* and 'A Portrait of the Artist', he devised the name for *Ulysses* himself and kept the title *Finnegans Wake* a secret for nearly twenty years.)

There is no evidence in the novel that Stephen's future involves Trieste, Zürich or Paris, however much we might wish to have him follow in Joyce's footsteps. In fact, it seems to be an essential quality of Stephen that he is a partial representation of Joyce and of Joyce only up to a particular date. The *Portrait* ends, decisively, with Stephen about to leave Ireland. *Ulysses* ends after Stephen has met Bloom but it does not (our wishful thinking aside) show him finding a demonstrably purposive future. He walks out of the book before the end and Joyce has been scrupulously careful to cut off his known lines of possible retreat; he will not return to the tower, or to his father's house: 'I will not sleep here tonight. Home also I cannot go' (*U* 23). Stephen's decision in 'Proteus' not to visit the Gouldings may hint that he will not go to stay with them either and this suggestion seems particularly significant because when Joyce himself left the tower he did go to stay with the family on whom the Gouldings are based.

It also seems that Stephen and Mulligan are decisively estranged during the novel: some act of hostility occurs at Westland Row station. We cannot imagine Stephen returning to his job at Dalkey and not only because he has rashly offered it to Corley, of all people (*U* 617). It is remarkable, too, that Stephen scarcely thinks about the future in *Ulysses*, as though for him it does not exist. At the end of the novel he may go off to write a novel (but not *Ulysses*) or he may go off to drown himself. Support for either of those hypotheses could be gathered from the text. But neither hypothesis about his future — nor any other hypothesis — can be proved conclusively.

Another element of *Ulysses* which contributes to the characterisation of Stephen and helps to limit his role as an embodiment of his creator, is the inclusion in the novel of ideas of his own. We need to consider how this method of characterisation works.

In the *Portrait*, as we have seen, Stephen's aesthetic pronouncements function as part of his characterisation and also as a means by which Joyce can comment obliquely on the nature of literary characterisation in general. In *Ulysses*, the closest parallel to those aesthetic pronouncements is Stephen's Shakespeare theory, which concerns the relationship between author and character and which also helps to depict Stephen's character for us. The theory is the most explicit treatment of author-character relationships anywhere in Joyce's works (which does not, of course, mean that it should be taken as a direct expression of Joyce's opinion). The central position of the Shakespeare discussion in *Ulysses* and the fact that it constitutes the last sustained expression of Stephen's mind, as well as his last appearance without Bloom, give it considerable emphasis, despite some weaknesses in Stephen's theory (including his admission at the end of his exposition that he is sceptical about his own ideas).

Stephen's insistence that Shakespeare identified himself less with Hamlet than with Hamlet's father may hint that Joyce is now to be identified less with Stephen than with Bloom, as critics have suggested, yet this hint is more a tantalising possibility than a matter of fact. It is Stephen who, like the Ghost in *Hamlet*, wears 'the castoff mail of a court buck' (*U* 188), in the form of second-hand clothes given to him by the foppish Buck Mulligan (who, incidentally, gets elaborately dressed in 'Telemachus' in order to walk a few yards and undress again for swimming). Stephen aspires to Shakespeare's position himself and he stresses in this particular connection Shakespeare's supposed seduction by Ann Hathaway:

The greyeyed goddess who bends over the boy Adonis,
stooping to conquer, as prologue to the swelling act, is
a boldfaced Stratford wench who tumbles in a cornfield
a lover younger than herself.
And my turn? When? (*U* 191).

This is Stephen's most explicit acknowledgment of the form
his incompleteness takes. Stephen attributes to Shakespeare
sexual problems which resemble Bloom's but also echo his
own.

Stephen teasingly, if unknowingly, offers comment on
Joyce's own autobiographical work. His remark that
Shakespeare 'wrote the play in the months that followed
his father's death' (*U* 207) might remind us that Joyce
wrote *Stephen Hero* in the months that followed his mother's
death and permit or encourage us to seek significance in that
fact. For example, Joyce felt obliged to take over the
function of guarding his own past, a task which his mother
had performed for him while she was alive. In both cases,
Joyce's and Shakespeare's, the literary work was a response
to the death of a parent and could not have been written
while that parent was still alive (if we accept Stephen's
argument). Joyce would not have made the association so
explicitly, but by having Stephen make it he allows us to
apply it to his own situation as well as Shakespeare's.
Stephen seeks out autobiographical associations throughout
Shakespeare's works:

— As for his family, Stephen said, his mother's name lives in
the forest of Arden. Her death brought from him the scene
with Volumnia in *Coriolanus* [here again, the preoccupation
with the literary consequences of the death of a parent
has implications for Stephen and Joyce as well as for
Shakespeare]. His boyson's death is the deathscene of
young Arthur in *King John*. Hamlet, the black prince, is
Hamnet Shakespeare. Who the girls in *The Tempest*, in
Pericles, in *Winter's Tale* are we know. Who Cleopatra,
fleshpot of Egypt, and Cressid and Venus are we may
guess (*U* 208).

These equations are, of course, too simple, as the unqualified
statement 'Joyce is Stephen' would also be too simple. It is

tempting to construct for *Ulysses* a list parallel to Stephen's: 'Joyce's mother's death brought from him Stephen's guilt; Rudy Bloom is the Joyces' stillborn child; Molly is Nora'. The partially unsatisfactory nature of these identifications casts doubt on Stephen's analysis. The *Portrait*-like irony directed at Stephen here is that Stephen himself (a partial and partly repudiated version of Joyce) is capable of less direct and less complete identification with his creator than he himself attempts to impose on Shakespeare's characters.

Stephen's conclusion, which he utters only on prompting from Eglinton, applies to *Ulysses* in a way Stephen is not placed to understand: 'The boy of act one is the mature man of act five. All in all. In *Cymbeline*, in *Othello* he is bawd and cuckold. He acts and is acted on. . . . His unremitting intellect is the hornmad Iago ceaselessly willing that the moor in him shall suffer' (*U* 212). Joyce, similarly, is present in both Stephen and Bloom and it is Joyce's equally unremitting intellect which chooses to explore through them his own kinds of vulnerability.

Thus Stephen's opinions do contain a degree of truth in relation to both himself and Joyce; but Stephen does not admit they apply to himself and does not know they apply to Joyce. Moreover, the opinions are outdistanced by the novel which contains them, as if to prove the inadequacy of using formulae to assess complex relationships. There is a simple but striking contrast between the method used to present Stephen's ideas in the *Portrait* and that used in *Ulysses*. In the *Portrait* his pronouncements appear near the end of the novel; but in *Ulysses* two-thirds of the action still lies ahead when he divulges his theory. Thus his ideas are exposed to more sustained ironic qualification in the later novel; subsequent episodes upset many of the certainties which the previous ones seem to establish and Stephen's theory, placed near the end of the more naturalistic part of the work, delineates the terms of this process of dissolution. The central irony is that for all his ingenuity in devising and expounding his theory, Stephen fails to see its relevance to his own situation, or to other aspects of life with which *Ulysses* concerns itself.

Immediately after Stephen's discussion of Shakespeare

he sees Bloom but fails to appreciate the ways in which Bloom relates to what he has been saying. For all its sophistication, then, the Shakespeare theory appears a little naïve when set against the weight of experience which is to follow it in the novel. But just as we feel that Stephen must exist in order for Bloom to exist, so the Shakespeare theory must be formulated in order that the imaginative complexities of the later episodes may have something against which to react.

The inadequacies of Stephen's theory are ultimately less intellectual than imaginative. It is insufficient, Joyce warns, to equate any character with his author or any author with his character, or to seek in such identifications the sole meaning of a literary work. But critics of Joyce must also accept the corollary: such issues are too important to overlook. What we must do is treat them carefully. Joyce can no more fuse with Stephen or Bloom than they can fuse with one another, or Shakespeare with Hamlet's father, for example. Stephen himself qualifies his theory, denying that he takes it seriously — though he presents his material earnestly enough despite the disclaimer — and, in 'Eumaeus', blithely undercutting that substantial portion of the theory which, like explanations of *Exiles* above, depended on names: 'Shakespeares were as common as Murphies. What's in a name?' (*U* 622). Joyce's own questioning of the value of Stephen's ideas is more radical. The latter stages of *Ulysses* treat issues which for Joyce may have become more important than his characters, though our knowledge of the characters' consciousnesses remains essential to Joyce's way of treating those issues. Such matters will include the difficulty of affirmation and of communication, coupled with the need to attempt them.

Thus in the *Portrait*, Stephen expressed theories which reflected his own experiences in ways he himself did not acknowledge, an irony which in turn demonstrated what Stephen had left out of the theories: some recognition of the effects of experience on modes of thought. In *Ulysses*, Stephen has advanced, in the sense that he now acknowledges the importance of experience in the creation of artistic works. Yet he still fails to apply his thoughts adequately to his own situation. He has moved from a theory detached from broad human experience and also from himself to one which is closer to broad human experience but still detached from himself. For all his continued self-preoccupation, then, Stephen still does not manage to fit himself into his environment, even while his sense of that environment has, in itself, become more sophisticated. Stephen still functions in some ways as a negative example, despite such promising signs as his mature 'Parable of the Plums' or his narrative of an imaginary visit to the Gouldings. But Stephen's meaning in this novel is no longer something he seems able to control, as he largely could in the *Portrait*. His meaning now depends on that new element in Joyce's world: a very different character, Leopold Bloom.

II: *Bloom*

Just as we settle into another 'novel about Stephen', the most startling change of direction anywhere in Joyce's work occurs: Mr Leopold Bloom makes his first appearance. He appears just when Stephen seems to have established his independence, in 'Proteus', and sets against the intellectual tension of that episode the appetite which is the first quality attributed to him: 'Mr Leopold Bloom ate with relish the inner organs of beasts and fowls' (*U* 54–5).

We find that we are to stay with Bloom through most of a long day and that he is more interesting than that taste in food, in itself, might lead us to expect. Yet the taste in food is an important counterweight to Stephen's ethereal speculations, his contempt for the body. Bloom has considerable gravitational force; the whole novel, after seeming attached to Stephen, begins to orbit around Bloom. Humbly, unknowingly but quite inexorably, Bloom takes over the book.

The initial contrast with Stephen could not be more striking. Stephen is prepared for, his past charted in the *Portrait*, his intellectual forebears described for us, his life and interests close enough to Joyce's (to relax for a moment into a lazy formulation) that we know approximately what to expect from him. For Bloom we are totally unprepared. He is outside our scheme of things, as he is outside Stephen's.

And he does not merely follow Stephen in the text, he supplants him. 'So portentous is Bloom's appearance that the sun in the sky is set back, and the day of *Ulysses* commences over again at 8 a.m.'[4] Only when we have met Bloom as well as Stephen can the day advance further. *Ulysses* also seems to state that Stephen needs to understand Bloom before he can advance further himself; but that conclusion is more problematic.

From further reading — either in *Ulysses* itself or in books about it — we learn to see Bloom in relation to Odysseus and so acknowledge belatedly that the novel's title should have led us to expect him. We find out, or recall, what Joyce said to Frank Budgen about Odysseus: that he was a rich and satisfying character because he appeared simultaneously in a range of relationships, as son, father, husband, lover and so on. Bloom is seen in terms of such a variety of relationships too, but in his case they are all heavily qualified (his father a suicide, his son dead, his wife unfaithful, his daughter apparently straying, his 'lovers' only the dusty, epistolary Martha Clifford and sugary, voyeuristic Gerty MacDowell). Yet Bloom is ennobled, made more Odysseus-like, because despite these apparent failures and the remorse some of them cause him (chiefly Molly's adultery, but also his father's suicide and the others to a lesser extent) he does continue to believe in relationships.

His involvement with those around him is hardly superior to Stephen's; in fact, in 'Aeolus' and especially 'Scylla and Charybdis' Stephen shows a degree of rapport with groups of people which Bloom never attains, something which is emphasised by Bloom's guilty and furtive appearances in both these episodes. Yet Bloom accepts the importance of engagement with other people, despite failure and trauma, while Stephen is intent on avoiding serious commitments of any kind.

This kind of qualification of Stephen is an obvious role of Bloom's. Bloom reveals the limitations imposed by Stephen's solipsism with a clarity Stephen himself never achieves and more emphatically because unconsciously.

Not all the points of contrast between Stephen and Bloom work in Bloom's favour; in fact, the two characters could have been put in a different novel designed to emphasise the superiority of Stephen. But in *Ulysses* as it stands, stress usually falls on Bloom's possession of qualities which Stephen lacks. The first six episodes set the two men in elaborate, pointed opposition. Bloom's black clothes, which he wears while in mourning for a man he hardly knows, show a social concern, one which is reinforced by his charitable acts on behalf of the Dignams and only slightly qualified by Molly's information that Bloom likes funerals and would willingly go into mourning for the cat. Bloom had attended Mrs Sinico's funeral, and from 'A Painful Case' it is difficult to imagine that she would have had many mourners; if Bloom knew the circumstances of her death he might have associated her with his father, another person who apparently died partly from loneliness and thus have been led to sympathise with her.

Stephen's 'cheap dusty mourning' (*U* 18) does emphasise his brooding regret and remorse over his mother's death, emotions with which we may sympathise, but it also has a literary, self-advertising quality which is less attractive particularly when contrasted with Bloom's more practical demeanour (though it is possible to argue that Bloom, too, is advertising his own distress by wearing mourning).

While both Bloom and Stephen are 'keyless', exiled in Dublin and wandering the streets for much of the day, Stephen's key would admit him only to the tower where he is oppressed by Mulligan, while Bloom's key would admit him to his home and Molly's ample bedwarmed flesh. Bloom's professed irritation with himself for forgetting the key should not disguise the possibility that, at least subconsciously, he wants to leave it behind to make a statement, to give poignancy to his partly wilful exclusion from Molly's favours. But it is more certain that Stephen's masochistic insistence on his own usurpation gains explicit support from Mulligan's retention of the tower key. It is appropriate that in 'Telemachus' we see Stephen leave the tower resolving never to return, while in 'Calypso' we see Bloom leaving his home temporarily (to buy food) and returning; we have here in microcosm a comparison of their movements during the day, since Stephen never does go back to the tower while

Bloom will, ultimately, return home.

Similarly, while both men must deal with usurpers, Bloom's intellectual victory over Boylan can be cautiously deduced from Molly's monologue, whereas Stephen's final position in relation to Mulligan remains unresolved. The difference between Stephen and Bloom appears most poignantly when we reflect that Bloom does have Molly (to some extent) while Stephen has nobody (or nobody but Mulligan). Both Stephen and Bloom play the role of servant; Stephen calls himself one and we first see Bloom serving Molly breakfast. But uxorious Bloom is a more willing servant than embittered Stephen, as Molly is a worthier object of service than Mulligan.

Bloom qualifies Stephen in a further, more direct way. Stephen, priding himself on his insight and his ability to read the 'signatures of all things' (*U* 37), nevertheless makes little of Bloom. All the time the two are together in 'Eumaeus' and 'Ithaca' we sense painfully that Stephen appreciates Bloom far less than Bloom believes or wishes, or than we ourselves might wish. (There are a few, sometimes touching, exceptions, as when Stephen endorses Bloom's dislike of violence [*U* 643], probably a more important agreement than the later one about 'the influence of gaslight or electric light on the growth of adjoining paraheliotropic trees' [*U* 667].)

Stephen remains with Bloom during this time more because he is exhausted and depressed than because he sees Bloom in particular as special. The wry disappointment thus induced in readers who have come to know and like Bloom is a vital aspect of that infusion of sympathy which *Ulysses* encourages. Even in earlier parts of the novel, Stephen's ignorance of Bloom's situation contrasts sharply with the observations of otherwise less perceptive people; it seems at times, though the impression may be largely due to Bloom's fears, that many people in Dublin suspect Molly of adultery — but not Stephen, who knows nothing about Molly at all. More subtly, part of Stephen's appeal for Bloom may be Bloom's sense that Stephen is ignorant of what has been going on in the Bloom household during the day.

This impression of Stephen's early failure to acknowledge Bloom receives its sharpest endorsement when Mulligan warns Stephen about the threat Bloom poses to his integrity

(Bloom will later reciprocate, with more justification, in warning Stephen about Mulligan). Mulligan maliciously, though without expecting to convince, misrepresents the nature of the threat, presenting as a homosexual motive what will be basically a desire for friendship and moral support; but Mulligan's warning does accord with what we know of Bloom's absorption in his own problems and the consequent danger that he will subordinate another person's emotional needs to his own. (It also ironically echoes Stephen's fear that Mulligan's own motivation may be homosexual.) If even Mulligan manages such an insight into Bloom's mind, however slight his real knowledge or interest, Stephen's failure to understand Bloom must seem especially glaring. It is also possible that Mulligan's warning has indeed prejudiced Stephen against Bloom, particularly through the reminder that Bloom knows Simon Dedalus (*U* 201). Stephen's 'black panther vampire' (*U* 608), though an almost subconscious muttering, conveys to us his fear that Bloom may be a predator, and the 'black panther' recalls Haines and hence Mulligan.

In Stephen's 'Parable of the Plums', a pleasant short story implicitly composed to evoke and encourage his own interest in his fellow-citizens, Stephen deals with people about whom he knows little or nothing. Though in the story he shows imagination and skill in depicting the lives of Anne Kearns and Florence MacCabe, he might do better to study someone like Leopold Bloom who is near at hand and whose life offers kinds of interest which Stephen seems ill-equipped to notice but should learn to understand. Joyce is probably implying that Stephen will need to write about real people whom he knows well in order to become a successful author; that is, to adopt the kind of sympathetic naturalism which was one of Joyce's own strengths.

The structure of the novel's first six episodes encourages us to compare Stephen and Bloom and so to construct from the novel a world, approximately resembling the actual Dublin, in which characters who have little contact with one another can coexist. Our interest in this process, which is quite new in Joyce, draws attention away from a relationship we might otherwise have investigated first: that between Bloom and Joyce.

It has been claimed that 'Bloom is exactly as autobiographical as Stephen'.[5] This proposition is startling: Stephen seems to have a monopoly on the factual details of Joyce's life, at least the details of 1904. But a comparison between Molly and Nora stresses the affinity between the Bloom household and the Joyce household as it was when the novel was being written; in each family, too, there have been a son and a daughter. We may notice, moreover, that Joyce and Bloom are about the same age: that is, Joyce reached Bloom's *Ulysses* age, thirty-eight, in 1920 as he brought the book towards completion. More significant may be the fact that Bloom married when he was twenty-two, Stephen's present age and Joyce's age when he met Nora. A vital contrast between Stephen and Bloom is this biographical one in which both are linked precisely to Joyce: Bloom and Joyce find life-partners at twenty-two, Stephen (despite his affinities with Joyce) apparently does not.

Bloom seems to take over from Stephen a responsibility for those aspects of Joyce's life which Nora made possible for him and to reflect amusingly on Joyce's surprisingly ordinary domestic side after the youthful rebel became something more like a 'simple middle-class man' (*JJ* 6) than he himself might have anticipated. Some readers might find it a significant point of contrast between Joyce and Bloom that Bloom had actually married Molly and Joyce had not married Nora (he did so much later and for practical reasons). But this contrast is required by Bloom's more complacent and accepting nature, not to mention his residence in conservative Dublin. At the same time Bloom's avoidance of his wedding as a topic for reflection, in this novel where he broods about so many things and especially matters involving Molly, may show not only his own sensitivity and discontent where Molly is concerned but also Joyce's reluctance to project into the life of a sympathetic character an event which he had banned in his own life.

Bloom has other attributes which resemble, or subtly parallel, aspects of Joyce. Ellmann observes that Joyce's 1909 letters to Nora show 'traces of fetishism, anality, paranoia, and masochism' (*SL* xxv) — all traits which have parallels in Bloom's character and are highlighted luridly in his treatment in the 'Circe' episode. Bloom's Jewishness, agnosticism and rootlessness parallel in a quietly positive and creative way Joyce's dislike of the oppression imposed by church and state in Ireland. England and Catholicism are linked as oppressors in Stephen's conversation with Haines in 'Telemachus', the first serious discussion in the novel; English authority and anti-Semitic sentiment are linked through Mr Deasy. Bloom's good-natured, calm incomprehension of the Catholic rituals in 'Hades' parallels Joyce's later attitude by distancing the observer from the ritual, depriving the Church of the power to threaten while retaining an appreciation of its aesthetic qualities and acknowledging the harsh realities which religion may palliate but cannot remove.

R. M. Adams has expressed this use of Bloom's religious background more daringly: 'Bloom's Jewishness served, for Joyce, as a vehicle for his own self-pity; his moral complacency; his loneliness; his deep sense of sexual injury; his guilt; his self-loathing.'[6] This list is perturbing not only because such psychological speculations are questionable but because it is difficult to see so positive a character as Bloom emerging from such a psychic jungle as Adams describes. Yet 'knowing where to stop' in this kind of analysis is a recurring difficulty which needs to be admitted.

Bloom's cuckoldry seemingly dramatises Joyce's erroneous (if largely self-induced) fears of Nora's infidelity. The parallel between Joyce's relationship with Marthe Fleischmann and Bloom's with Martha Clifford is clear enough, though Bloom's 'affair' at the stage shown in *Ulysses* seems considerably more detached than Joyce's apparently was. Marthe Fleischmann's limp is bestowed not on Martha Clifford, who never appears except in her letter (where her syntax, admittedly, is limp) but on Gerty MacDowell; Bloom wonders momentarily if Martha and Gerty might be the same person — a theory which the limp might seem to substantiate, but only if we bring Joyce into the equations. It now seems that Gerty was named after another girlfriend of Joyce's, a connection which further supports the soundness of Bloom's judgement.[7] Again, Bloom's urbane remark about Martha's letter, 'Wonder did she wrote it herself' (*U* 78) recalls Nora's early practice, which irked Joyce, of copying letters to her lover out of a book.[8] Joyce, the great word-shaper, expected more original responses than that; later he would retaliate by borrowing some of Nora's expressions for his own books.

Nevertheless, the claim that Stephen and Bloom are 'equally' autobiographical, especially if taken to mean that they are autobiographical in the same way, threatens to undermine the significance of the contrast between them. It might even make their coexistence in the same work seem redundant, or narcissistic, which it never seems when we actually read the novel. Joyce does bestow aspects of himself on Bloom to emphasise support for him. But it is too simple to say that Stephen is young Joyce and Bloom is middle-aged Joyce. This is a formulation which the Stephen of the Shakespeare theory might devise himself if he were studying a novel like *Ulysses*. Stephen as he appears in *Ulysses* could grow into a person approximately resembling Joyce in the present, though there is no direct evidence in the novel to prove that he will and differences between them make the hypothesis problematic. But Bloom was never a Stephen, or a young Joyce. He has come from a different background and in the present he has reached a different resting-place. If Joyce feels more affection for Bloom than for Stephen, this is partly because Bloom is more distinct from himself, more a created character in his own right.

The mere fact that Bloom has other important models apart from Joyce confirms that he is a different kind of character from Stephen. The only living model for Stephen, apart from Joyce himself, is his brother Stanislaus; and Stanislaus in life performed exactly this kind of function as a foil or whetstone by means of which Joyce could define his own position more precisely. Stanislaus' appearance in the novel as a model for certain of Stephen's traits is thus less a compounding of Stephen's real-life origins than an accurate fictional representation of his actual role in Joyce's life.

But Bloom does owe some of his traits to other living people such as Italo Svevo. We need not consider the precise mechanics of these borrowings which have been extensively analysed by Ellmann. The vital point is that Bloom is based firmly on other people as well as on Joyce. Less important than the identity of particular sources is Joyce's willingness to play a diminished role in a central character. (It also seems likely that Richard Rowan in *Exiles*, the work Joyce had to finish before he could devote himself to *Ulysses*, absorbs precisely those aspects of Joyce himself which will not be needed for the portrait of Bloom.) Part of Bloom's significance is thus amplified by an awareness of his multiple sources: he embodies an acknowledgment of the complementary nature of the experiences of various people, thus enacting the fusion of diverse materials which it is one aim of *Ulysses* to bring about.

One amusing affinity between Bloom and Joyce remains to be discussed. Bloom is permitted to have a touch of the artist about him and one of his roles in the novel is as a contributor to the development of its narrative texture. If Stephen is an aesthete who has yet to become an artist, Bloom is a kind of artist *manqué*. His trade, canvasser for advertisements, reminds us of Stephen's (and, presumably, Joyce's) strictures on the 'kinetic' arts, of which advertising is surely a prime example. The book which most moves Bloom in *Ulysses*, though it does so by causing his already preoccupied mind to dwell on his own sexual problems, is a work of pornography, also kinetic in Stephen's definition.

Nevertheless, Bloom has intended to write out for publication a collection of Molly's sayings, using a method of literary research also employed by Joyce (Molly, amusingly, has contemplated performing the same favour for Bloom). In 'Circe' Bloom imagines himself composing something like *Dubliners*: 'I follow a literary occupation. Author-journalist. In fact we just bringing out a collection of prize stories of which I am the inventor, something that is an entirely new departure' (*U* 458). In 'Eumaeus' Bloom contemplates writing 'something out of the common groove ... *My Experiences*, let us say, *in a Cabman's Shelter*' (*U* 647), a title which would suit 'Eumaeus' itself if the chapter were in fact narrated by Bloom. The art Bloom produced might always be inadequate, but he does qualify Stephen's artistic aspirations by his endlessly curious engagement in life, which contrasts with Stephen's aloofness.

Bloom's curiosity on Bloomsday admittedly owes something to his desire to distract himself from events at home, but that does not invalidate it: Joyce never idealises any human emotion or impulse, even curiosity. Bloom has some of the introspection and narrative slyness of the Joycean writer and he has an autobiographical habit which leads him to repeated recapitulations of the events of his day and also of his more distant past. Joyce uses Bloom's consciousness in the central episodes of *Ulysses* as he had used Stephen's in the *Portrait* and the Telemachiad and as he will use Molly's in 'Penelope'. What we see in 'Calypso', for example, is governed not only by what Bloom sees but by the way he sees it: thus particular emphasis falls on Molly's unattractiveness at a time when Bloom is trying to reconcile himself to the impending fact of her engagement with Boylan, or to his own complicity in that liaison and the guilt which this complicity causes.

In episodes like 'Calypso', then, or 'Lestrygonians', Bloom's perceptions affect the point of view and even the narrative technique. Here we reach and must explore more directly a mode of characterisation which Joyce develops fully for the first time in *Ulysses*: the manipulation of the relationship between the characters and the novel's methods of narration.

III: *Narration*

Joyce's experimentation with treatments of character in *Ulysses* is richer in many respects than anything in his earlier works. One aspect which will strike readers of *Ulysses* almost immediately is the internal angle of narration.

This method can be conveniently called 'stream of consciousness'. The term provokes critical debate but since only one novel is in question here and the novel clearly seeks to represent the consciousness of its central characters, the general appropriateness of such terms need not cause anxiety. Readers will agree about what is meant. The point is that such techniques, unknown earlier in Joyce, become vital in the opening episodes of *Ulysses* and dominate much of the novel. They inevitably affect our perception of the characters.

Even in *Dubliners* and the *Portrait*, the narrative reproduced closely the rhythms of the characters' consciousnesses. In the case of the *Portrait*, little critical harm results from envisaging a single narrator and equating him with Stephen himself. No event takes place which is inaccessible to Stephen and the diary at the end is ascribed directly to him, as if a gradual or intermittent fusion of narrator and character has taken place throughout the novel. One reason for our ready assimilation of the stream-of-consciousness technique in *Ulysses* is this previous rapprochement of narrator's and character's minds. Yet nowhere before *Ulysses* does Joyce abandon the pretence of constant external narrative presence — even if, as in the *Portrait*, the narrator is 'external' to his own younger self, rather than that of a separate character.

What happens early in *Ulysses*, then, is that an apparently omniscient narrative gives place, intermittently but increasingly, to direct transcriptions of the characters' consciousnesses. There are striking divergences here from Joyce's earlier practices.

In *Dubliners* and the *Portrait*, the narrative seemed to be constitutionally neutral, but to imitate the characters' patterns of thoughts and speech as an economical way of indicating their nature to us. If in the *Portrait* narrator and character are the 'same' person, this imitation shows a kind of narcissism which is quite appropriate in that novel but it is not structurally different from the narrative modes of *Dubliners*. Hence, perhaps, the coolness, balance and suspension of judgment which have perturbed some readers of the *Portrait*. We do not expect to achieve such coolness in inspecting our own past; but Joyce had practised his detachment in *Dubliners* first.

In *Ulysses*, the narrative makes much less apparent effort to 'imitate' the consciousnesses of the characters. This point has two main implications, one involving Stephen and the other involving Bloom. Molly is a special case, because her monologue is transcribed directly, without narrative intrusions (even the representations of the sounds of passing trains are not supplied by a narrator: they are in the text solely because they register in Molly's mind).

In the case of Stephen, the narrative seems capable of

making judgments closely resembling those of the character and equalling them in intelligence and insight. This resemblance is reinforced by the language; Stephen's thoughts and the narrative are expressed in similar tones, marked by verbal dexterity and erudition and transitions between narrative and Stephen's stream of consciousness are therefore effortless: 'Stephen bent forward and peered at the mirror held out to him, cleft by a crooked crack, hair on end. As he and others see me. Who chose this face for me? This dogsbody to rid of vermin. It asks me too' (*U* 6). Yet this is not the technique of the *Portrait*. Because the events of *Ulysses* are confined to one day, we do not sense the developing, retrospective narrative attention which marked the earlier work. There is no narrator 'imitating' a younger self but a more impersonal narrative resembling in tone the discourse of a present self. None of the effort to attain an attitude, discernible in the early works, appears in *Ulysses*.

In the second aspect, the case of Bloom, the difference from Joyce's earlier works is still more striking. It is a commonplace of *Ulysses* criticism that the narrative through which Bloom is presented sometimes attains a felicity of word and phrase which Bloom himself could never manage. For the first time in Joyce, a character's thoughts are presented in a form beyond the grasp of the character. At times, as in Bloom's oriental fantasy in 'Calypso', the effect is a sympathetic enrichment of his consciousness. What was apparently present in Bloom's mind only as half-formed images becomes eloquently complete for us through narrative endowed with a sublety and articulateness Bloom lacks. Although Bloom's degree of self-knowledge seems inferior to Stephen's or Joyce's, the narrative of 'Calypso' does not attempt to supplement it. Moreover, information Bloom would be unable to share with us is generally omitted by the narrative too, though it is difficult to know in what degree this limitation is due to Bloom's own half-conscious suppression of facts (in the interests of heightening his masochistic feelings or eliciting our sympathy for him). We feel that Bloom would approve of the way he is presented at this stage of the novel if he were able to read it. Though he has probably not heard words like 'gelid' and 'felly', they are words he would enjoy if he did know them. The narrative thus creates a Bloomian atmosphere even when couched in terms Bloom would not be able to use himself.

On other occasions, however, this narrative articulateness is less helpful to Bloom, as in his fantasy in 'Wandering Rocks': 'Warmth showered gently over him, cowing his flesh. Flesh yielded amid rumpled clothes. Whites of eyes swooning up. His nostrils arched themselves for prey' (*U* 236). This passage conveys the pathos of Bloom's situation as cuckold but also his masochism and his susceptibility to slight erotic influences. In this case the narrative detachment and eloquence draw attention to Bloom's limitations rather than his strengths.

Perhaps this change in technique was necessary in order to keep such a large novel as *Ulysses* supple and dynamic: solidly presented characters brought to us by a narrator consistently concerned to imitate them might have produced a rigid work. The characters in *Ulysses* are capable of surprising us in ways unavailable to Joyce's earlier characters and this capability owes much to the new narrative methods. Imitative narration prepares us for a character's normal mode of behaviour but the more oblique narrative of *Ulysses* does not. At the same time, we are now less exclusively dependent on the narrative for our information, since the characters provide much of it for us directly, and since the narrative, particularly in later stages of the novel, appears less reliable as a guide to the characters' experiences. For example, readers have assumed for years that the 'hallucinations' in 'Circe' appear to the characters; only recently have these visions been attributed instead to Joyce, the book or the reader, all more plausible candidates than the characters. The reader is probably the best candidate of all.

The new methods thus deprive the reader of certainties, of easy readings of the characters. It is a much more challenging exercise now to assess them: we have to balance what they show us themselves with what we are told about them and neither of these impressions is in itself concrete or definitive. In later parts of the novel this puzzle continues to intensify, as we acquire more and more information about the characters (we probably learn as much about Bloom in

'Ithaca' as in all sixteen previous episodes combined) but their actual nature or importance becomes ever harder to define. Just as we believe we have grasped essential facts about the characters, there is a strategic narrative withdrawal or a newly perplexing complication of textual surface.

The impossibility of fully knowing a person thus emerges almost as a theme of *Ulysses* — with negative implications if we think such knowledge fully attainable and desirable, but with positive ones if we find the quest for such knowledge continuously interesting, with an interest which would be lost if certainty could be achieved. Our curiosity about the characters helps to hold *Ulysses* together and keeps us reading through the difficulties of the later episodes; it might be difficult to enjoy 'Oxen of the Sun' at all if characters we already knew were not at least present in it. Although it is true that the characters seem to 'recede' from us in some of the later episodes, as authorial attention ranges elsewhere, this method is only feasible because we have approached the characters so closely in earlier chapters. If we had not become familiar with them we would not care that they are receding.

Like many questions about Joyce's work, this relationship between character and technique can also be profitably approached from the opposite direction. If Joyce's wish to show character as enigmatic demands subtle, complex and sometimes obfuscating styles, it can also be argued that the styles he chooses to use determine the kinds of characters he can depict.

For a novel of its length and complexity *Ulysses* has very few 'central' characters. We can claim to know intimately only Stephen and Bloom, since theirs are the only minds to which we have extensive access; we do find out about Molly as well, but only in the final episode, so that she is kept enigmatic as we read earlier sections of the book. This effect survives even into subsequent readings of the text, as the information available to be gleaned in 'Penelope' is not distributed through the early chapters; we are unlikely to have Molly's monologue recalled to mind by details in those chapters. We gain admittance occasionally and briefly to other minds, but always those of minor characters like Gerty

MacDowell, Father Conmee and Master Patrick Dignam. None of these characters is presented through stream-of-consciousness methods in more than one episode; Gerty's mind is presented obliquely, probably to emphasise her coyness and one such character, the 'Cyclops' narrator, is anonymous. Even Molly's mind is depicted from within only in one episode. We hear nothing in the novel of the workings of Mulligan's mind, he being all surfaces, or of Simon Dedalus' mind, perhaps because he is alienated from Stephen and of Boylan's thoughts we hear only three words.

Stephen and Bloom, besides sharing the stage as the novel's only central characters, share their physical passivity, present unhappiness, isolation, alienation, introspection and interest in language, qualities which lend themselves perfectly to stream-of-consciousness narration. Such narration at length may only be possible where characters think and brood copiously, spend considerable time alone and find relationships with others difficult and have sufficient imagination to make their thoughts seem varied and interesting (or a narrator who will supply them with such thoughts — but Joyce never uses this method, as Virginia Woolf sometimes seems to do). Stream-of-consciousness characters need preoccupations or obsessions to give their thoughts a strong central current, but also the energy and ingenuity to try out various ways of overcoming those obsessions.

Bloom, in addition, is not publicly articulate except on rare occasions, so that his most fluent thoughts remain thoughts without being expressed to others; this is another attribute which the stream-of-consciousness technique — resulting in our familiarity with aspects of Bloom which are not disclosed to the people around him — tends to accentuate. Although he lacks Stephen's education, Bloom is interested in the way language works, as he is interested in the way everything works. This is a further attribute which stream-of-consciousness technique, in its own interests, acts to reinforce. Although we think of Bloom as wordy, he never actually says a great number of words in our hearing: much of his verbal activity remains, as noted above, internal and unexpressed. Apart from 'Circe', which clearly contains many words nobody 'really' said, Bloom speaks about four thousand words in *Ulysses*. But more than half of these appear in 'Eumaeus', where Bloom's talk is particularly flabby and redundant, mostly addressed to a sleepy, drunk, slightly concussed auditor who is present out of apathy and exhaustion more than anything else. Bloom probably intends his talk in this episode to soothe Stephen and prevent him from leaving.

In only three other episodes does Bloom produce more than three hundred words. Of these he is most eloquent in 'Aeolus' and 'Cyclops'; in both these cases he is particularly oppressed and belittled and his eloquence does nothing but get him into trouble. Another point to emerge from this analysis is that a different and slightly more positive impression of Bloom emerges if we concentrate on his speeches, perhaps because in those speeches his social virtues, like gentleness and generosity, appear most clearly. Nevertheless, the 'sense of Bloom' we are meant to perceive is, of course, one which results from the interaction between Bloom's own thoughts and words and the narrative: we may have to remind ourselves occasionally that he is not a real person but a function of all the means Joyce uses to depict him.

It is also true that to undergo successfully the narrative modes Joyce employs later in *Ulysses*, characters need staying power, versatility and some sense of humour; continued subjection and exposure to such narrative modes will tend to accentuate these attributes. We respect a character's resilience simply because the character has remained sane through 'Circe', alert through 'Eumaeus', human through 'Ithaca'. Joyce introduces us to this method through a relatively straightforward example, 'Cyclops', where we respect Bloom for remaining reasonable and peaceful despite his unruly and bellicose company. The narrative techniques of the later episodes emphasise details of character which we already know or assume to exist, but they also determine what kinds of characters can be presented.

At the end of the novel Bloom and Stephen seem special partly because they have survived the extraordinary narrative ordeal Joyce has forced them to undergo. It is hard to imagine other characters, whether those of *Ulysses* or those of different novels, coping with such trials. Characters so

created and depicted are bound to seem strong and Stephen
and Bloom do acquire before the end of the novel a strength
which they earlier lacked. All the narrative and stylistic
'reductions' which *Ulysses* attempts and which qualify points
of detail, do not finally suppress the characters.

Bloom suffers this process of reduction more severely
than Stephen and is, accordingly, more emphatically vindicated by surviving it. Bloom is the main target partly because
he plays a larger role in the later episodes than Stephen does
(which in turn shows that Joyce now finds Bloom more
interesting than Stephen) and partly because the narrative
attacks exploit verbal strategies which Stephen is better
equipped than Bloom to counter. In 'Oxen of the Sun', for
example, Stephen would be capable of appreciating the
details of the stylistic parodies and imitations which seem to
reduce the individual characters even while they create an
abstractly humane atmosphere. In fact, Stephen's literary
interests and sense of style might well enable him to write
parodies approaching the quality of those in 'Oxen', though
it is not suggested here that he is in fact doing so. Bloom,
by contrast, would not recognise most of the authors who
are imitated and would not be capable of writing any part
of the episode. Bloom is conspicuously more ill at ease in
this highly verbal chapter than Stephen is, just as he was in
the previous highly verbal chapters 'Aeolus' and 'Scylla
and Charybdis'. The effect of the stylistic convolutions of
'Oxen', then, is to restrict Bloom more than Stephen.

This pattern does not last until the end of the novel,
however. If 'Oxen' (or 'Cyclops' or 'Circe') shows Bloom in
a negative light, there are also signs of an attempt to redeem
him — signs which become more pronounced in 'Eumaeus'
and 'Ithaca'. The style of 'Eumaeus' — seemingly a parody of
Bloom's own style — ought to make him appear ridiculous,
but in fact emphasises the positive qualities of Bloom's
habits of thought: his resilience, his curiosity, his equanimity.
'Ithaca' similarly discloses the intellectual flabbiness Bloom
sometimes displays but also demonstrates his eclectic interests,
his curiosity (again) and his humanitarianism. Since 'Ithaca'
contains no direct speech, Stephen's verbal fluency does not
give him such an advantage here as previously. We sense that

Bloom has won out, simply by enduring, simply by being Bloom. He parries stylistic and narrative thrusts as he shakes off blows of fate. Like Odysseus, he survives repeated ordeals; unlike Odysseus, he finds (having exchanged the violent classical Mediterranean for the most verbal city on earth) that his ordeals usually involve words rather than actions.

The relationship of character and narrative thus remains one of the most crucial aspects of *Ulysses*. Joyce takes characters based approximately on himself, but controls them by employing narrative methods equipped to treat them both intelligently and sternly. The result is an intriguing work which avoids the introspection or narcissism such a novel might have shown (and which, one could argue, appear in *Exiles*) by keeping the characters shrewdly and wittily in their place.

IV: *Ending*

Before leaving *Ulysses*, we must confront directly its crucial, enigmatic event, the meeting of Stephen and Bloom and the implications of this event for Joyce's treatment of character.

The meeting seems in many ways positive. Some sympathy appears between Stephen and Bloom, some hint that each is able for a moment to imagine and identify with the situation of the other (Bloom seems better at doing this than Stephen). Stephen, as a very young man, has life-determining decisions to make, while Bloom is at an age when choice tends to narrow down, when life is increasingly determined by the outcome of past choices. Both these stages are potentially difficult and each can learn from the other — one of Joyce's implications in his juxtaposition of them. Bloom may see in Stephen the possibility of new directions in the future while Stephen may see in Bloom the need to reconcile himself to his own past actions. More subtly, by a process of double reflection, Stephen may see the need to make decisions and Bloom the need to come to terms with choices made in the past.

While he is with Bloom Stephen does overcome, briefly and partially, his intense self-absorption and his impulse to reject and to flee. Bloom has an opportunity to act charitably, even paternally, towards Stephen. While some interpretations of the fatherhood theme in *Ulysses* have been too optimistic or even sentimental, the vision of Rudy which appears as Bloom watches over Stephen at the end of 'Circe' makes the 'paternity' interpretation inevitable, whether we think Bloom himself sees the vision or believe it is put in the text to illustrate to us that Bloom has had a twinge of paternal feeling. Bloom offers a stability and balance which Stephen lacks, qualities which are obliquely illustrated by the fact that Bloom's budget balances while Stephen's is all debit (*U* 31, 711). Bloom's human weaknesses, which cause a slight editing of his budget to disguise his visit to the brothel, do not invalidate these qualities, any more than his alleged willingness to wear mourning for the cat invalidates the genuine concern he shows by going to Dignam's funeral.

Such positive interpretations do receive support from imagistic and structural features of the novel's ending. The eucharistic implications of the cocoa-drinking of Stephen and Bloom have often been noted. The novel begins on a tower, emblematical of war and ends in a bed, emblematical of love; we move from the green sea of Stephen's melancholy brooding and his mother's cancerous bile to the red sea of Molly's euphoric recollections and her menstrual blood (admittedly a less unequivocally positive symbol but a necessary confirmation that she is not pregnant by Boylan and that there is therefore a possibility of a new pregnancy by Bloom). The novel moves from Mulligan, who denies, to Molly, who affirms. Much has been made of Molly's final 'Yes', apparently casting benign affirmation over the events of the ending but Stephen's last directly quoted word is also 'Yes' (*U* 660), an acceptance, albeit an uncertain one, of Bloom's invitation to Eccles Street.

There may be a buried pun in all the business about breakfast in bed: we feel that the Blooms need to end their evasion of potentially procreative sexuality, to break their 'fast' in bed. The last occasion when Bloom asked for breakfast in bed, we find, coincided with the period of Rudy's birth and death, the time when full sexual relations between Bloom and Molly came to an end. Molly's first utterance in the novel was a negative grunt in response to Bloom's question whether she wanted anything for breakfast (*U* 56); her final 'Yes' is, among other things, a response to his request that she should bring him his breakfast in bed next day. In her monologue Molly moves from pleased recollections of Boylan's sexual prowess to a recognition that Boylan has little except sexual prowess to offer and that Bloom is in most respects a superior being. Even if we cannot legitimately speculate about the events of the next day, we have some excuse for feeling that the Blooms are better off now than they were in the morning, that Bloom, in his vicarious fatherhood of Stephen, has directed himself towards Molly and the possibility of having a son.

Nevertheless, it is all too easy to enthuse about a 'positive' ending to a novel, especially one which has worked as hard as *Ulysses* has: *Ulysses* would seem to have earned the right to end positively if it wished to do so. It is clear (and has been said before) that Joyce did not write *Ulysses* in order to show the inferiority of a twentieth-century advertisement canvasser to a classical hero; but it may not follow from this fact that he wrote it to make the most positive statement which could possibly be made. It is strange to see some critics who have worked to disentangle the subleties and ambivalences of earlier episodes sit back and accept Molly's Yesses as the solution to everything.

Thus it is not surprising that some readings of the ending have reacted by becoming largely negative, as if Molly's Yes simply meant No. Bloom shows little explicit sign that he has been affected by his encounter with Stephen; indeed, it is remarkable just how little Bloom thinks about Stephen after the latter's departure. Stephen is less interested in Bloom than we feel he ought to be, certainly less interested than Joyce is — another mark of the divergence of author and character. Despite the breakfast request, Bloom still behaves towards Molly much as he usually does; if Joyce had wished to herald a return to full sexual relations between them, he need not have shown Bloom engaging in precisely those forms of sexual activity which Molly herself regards as a poor substitute for full relations. The request for breakfast may not have portentous implications — Bloom may simply feel exhausted, quite understandably and want one day's release from his usual morning routine as the provider of breakfast.[9]

The ending, viewed dispassionately, is more ambivalent than it first appears. There is no concrete evidence for any particular hypothesis about the events of 17 June. Stephen may be anywhere; he may have learnt something from his encounter with Bloom, or he may not. The Blooms may resume sexual relations in future, or they may not. Joyce said that the characters were off to eternity at the end of *Ulysses* and in his letters he expressed some exasperation with them. Yet these characters are more than a means of access to a significance they merely represent in passing: they are that significance. No novel stresses the uniqueness of each individual more than *Ulysses*, no novel is less concerned with establishing general truths. What the novel means depends precisely on what Joyce shows us about Stephen, Bloom and Molly. At the end these characters are withdrawn from our attention and we have only our recollections of their thoughts early in the novel by which to judge them. Any hints about the future are only hints. Bloom's youthful anagrams on his name (*U* 678) seem an impressionistic anticipation of his biography, but also suggest that the successive states of his life will be somewhat random and unpredictable rearrangements of his identity. His ideal future state, as imagined by himself, is at once implausible in its baroque domestic detail and a parodic version of his present condition rather than a real change from it.

Naturalistic interpretations of the ending, in terms of event or person, thus seem deficient. Yet the meeting of Stephen and Bloom is laden with implication. Does it involve only the implication that certainty is beyond our reach?

Interpretation of the novel's conclusion depends on the aspects of characterisation and the relationship between characterisation and narrative, which we have been considering.

Since both Stephen and Bloom partake of Joyce's own nature, their meeting seems bound to be uneasy. There is a certain skittishness, wariness and even evasion, particularly on Stephen's side, as when two like poles of magnets meet. There would be little point in bringing two aspects of Joyce together only to fuse them into an existing being resembling his present self; there is more point in the oscillating, punlike tension between two beings both similar and different who interact but do not combine.

The meeting of Stephen and Bloom juxtaposes a young man resembling Joyce in the past with an older man who combines aspects of Joyce developed since his Stephen days and aspects borrowed from other men. The meeting therefore implies that Stephen, like Joyce, should admit some possibility of change in himself, the acquisition of some Bloomian qualities and attributes like domesticity, paternity and equanimity. It also implies that Stephen, again like Joyce before him, should admit the kinship which exists between himself and other people. For the presentation of Stephen, we have seen, Joyce drew on his own past; for the presentation of Bloom he needed other models as well. These different origins amount to a vital distinction between Stephen and Bloom, analogous to the new facts which Stephen must himself confront. It is a requirement which he acknowledges in a theoretical manner earlier in the day: 'Dublin. I have much, much to learn' (*U* 144). When he meets Bloom, however, there is little sign that he sees him as an instance of this obligation.

Joyce thus dramatises some private admonitions but they also have public relevance which it is for his readers to notice. In this sense it may not matter that Stephen and Bloom seem to retain little from their encounter. Indeed, by analogy with the commonly accepted interpretation of *Ulysses* which argues that a reader's sympathy is aroused by narrative attacks on the characters, it might seem that the less meaning Stephen and Bloom take from the encounter, the more we will be led to take.

It may also be true that our external perspective leads us to see more in the meeting than Stephen and Bloom themselves could possibly see. We know far more about Stephen than Bloom does and far more about Bloom than Stephen does. We have more reason to wish success on their encounter than they have themselves: for them it may be just an encounter, but we have come to feel that on it may depend Bloom's future as a father and Stephen's future as a writer.

It is in this way that *Ulysses* becomes a novel about those who read it and creates the sensation that Joyce is appealing less because we come to understand him than because he comes to understand us. The encounter of Stephen and Bloom does become archetypal even while they retain their individual identities precisely; their meeting becomes a representation of the inconclusive encounters common in 'real life', in which unexpressed affinities may be felt more strongly than any planned or concrete outcome. Realising this, we should not feel disappointed that more does not result explicitly from the scene in *Ulysses*. Instead we might be grateful for a scene so cautiously, delicately presented, poised between the empty and the significant as so many real experiences are poised and also with that sense of elusive significance often evoked by conversations of the kind shown in 'Ithaca', taking place among people who are up late while most others are asleep. The meeting is, indeed, more satisfying because more full of possibility than it would be if its outcome were certain.

'Ithaca' achieves another kind of near-fusion as well. It brings together Bloom's interest in reality and Stephen's interest in ways of perceiving and describing reality – a dialectic enacted in the question-and-answer format of the episode. Put another way, it brings together the events of the novel and ways of understanding those events. These elements – the naturalistic core of the novel and methods of seeing it – have had a shifting and often perplexing relationship throughout *Ulysses*. The relationship is closest in 'Ithaca' and owing to the relative straightforwardness of Molly's mind it will remain close in 'Penelope'.

The ending of *Ulysses* thus shows the possibility of imaginative fusions between related states and between experience and ways of perceiving experience. The characters need not act out these fusions, or even be conscious of them. Yet the characters' presence and our knowledge of how they have been created remain essential to our full understanding of the processes dramatised in the novel's conclusion.

Argument over a 'positive' or 'negative' ending is thus partly beside the point. There is a studied neutrality about the ending which invites our participation in it, not to argue for one interpretation or another but simply to respond to its sense of rich possibility. The issuing of this invitation to us is Joyce's final deployment of Stephen, Molly and Bloom, none of whom will ever appear in his work again. They have been busy on this day, especially Stephen and Bloom (*Ulysses* cannot be an easy novel in which to appear as a character). Yet the characters do survive, do complete their assignment. In the end, the manner of their disappearance implies a confidence on Joyce's part that we have known them well and that our knowledge of them is vital. It is, we must remember, only in our imaginations that they retain any life at all.

Ultimately, Joyce believes quietly but insistently in the uniqueness of each individual, but also in the importance of the connections between people. He will not sentimentalise the relationship between these things. Only when the uniqueness is accepted, when the inalienable otherness of another person is acknowledged, can there be true communication. Joyce demonstrates this doctrine by bringing together two men who are intelligent and interested in words, creating an approximate balance between them by giving the intellectually less endowed one greater reserves of experience, but also showing the difficulties which arise when their communication is complicated by unresolved personal problems and by efforts (on Bloom's part, anyway) to seek too assiduously for points of resemblance. Stephen represents, from his first appearance in Joyce's works, Joyce's sense of the uniqueness of his own experience. Bloom represents Joyce's sense that the experience of each other person is also unique, but linked to his own by vivid analogies.

Yet for all this studied neutrality, Bloom is a remarkable addition to Joyce's fiction. The initially traumatic displacement of our attention caused by his first appearance in *Ulysses* will be vindicated by the extraordinary imaginative power which marks his presentation throughout the novel. Apparently inferior to Stephen in many ways and by conventional standards quite flawed, Bloom nevertheless comes to supplant Stephen in our estimation and to show the limitations of those conventional standards of judgment. Treated by a narrative which seems much better informed than he is and sometimes even hostile to him, Bloom endures with an indestructible dignity despite his many weaknesses. Bloom's diversity, his many-mindedness, his multiple family ties and his multiple sources combine to give him a three-dimensional solidity and resilience. In presenting Bloom in this way, Joyce is paying tribute both to the other men who provided traits for his hero and also to his own ingenuity in fusing those traits with aspects of his own personality to give Bloom a rich and fascinating character, impressive partly because of the sheer skill with which the ingredients have been combined.

It is as much a part of Bloom's meaning that he combines Joyce with other people as it is a part of Stephen's meaning that his sole important source is Joyce. The tension between Bloom and the narrative is a remarkable Joycean defence of his mature sense of community against the resources of his own art. The meeting of Stephen and Bloom enacts a vital process of Joycean awareness which is static in itself but capable of great promise if we are able to apprehend it. Yet, ultimately, Bloom rises above all the theorising. Joyce's most satisfying character, he exists partly to put in perspective the theories of people like Joyce critics, people whose behaviour Joyce, with his customary brilliance, fully anticipated. At a vital level, as Frank Budgen realised, the complexities recede and *Ulysses* remains a remarkable novel because it is about a remarkable character.

6

Finnegans Wake

One of the many problems posed by *Finnegans Wake* is the book's extraordinary ability to mimic the shape and strategy of any critical approach to it. We can find in the text almost anything we suspect it of containing and some published analyses show the ingenuity and persistence of critics in extracting possible meanings, rather than illuminating the ways in which Joyce actually worked. The book is both kaleidoscope ('collideorscape', *FW* 143.28) and mirror, seeming to dispose itself in patterns which we actually create ourselves and returning to us our own preoccupations.

Analysis of characterisation and especially of autobiographical characterisation cannot escape this danger altogether, particularly since the *Wake* sometimes presents its characters in unprecedented ways which critics may not even now be equipped to discuss. Characterisation in the *Wake* can become bewilderingly fluid and difficult to define. Nevertheless, inspection of an element of the text which is at once specific and general may at least avoid two further risks in *Wake* criticism — the considerable danger of not seeing the wood for the trees and on the other hand the danger of relying on simplifications which are of no help when we actually venture into the wood. Since characterisation has seemed an element particularly close to Joyce himself in all the earlier works, it can be hoped that an inspection of characterisation in the *Wake* will help to solve the puzzle of Joyce's attitude to the forms of communication attempted in his last work. Establishing what the characters are doing for Joyce may aid our understanding of what they are meant to be doing for us.

In discussing characterisation in the *Wake* we need to notice some qualifications expressed by Joyce himself. 'I ... am trying to tell the story of this Chapelizod family in a new way', he said. 'Time and the river and the mountain are the real heroes of my book. ... There is ... no connection between the people in *Ulysses* and the people in *Work in Progress*. There are in a way no characters. ... If one had to name a character, it would be just an old man. But his own connection with reality is doubtful' (*JJ* 554, 695—6). It is true that 'time and the river and the mountain' seem to function as characters; so, we might say, do words. But Dublin can be seen as a kind of character in *Ulysses*, and words seem to acquire personalities throughout Joyce's writing. The *Wake* is not an entirely new departure in its fertile use of personification. And though Joyce's human characters in the *Wake* are elusive, variable and prone to seem archetypal more than individual, it may still he helpful to observe the means Joyce uses to present them. They may be bundles of characteristics rather than distinct individuals, but literary characters are often created by an accumulation of traits; the real difference in the *Wake* may be that Joyce sometimes made little attempt to show the characters as plausible, unique personalities.

This kind of study proves particularly revealing, as throughout Joyce's work, where the traits in question clearly derive from his own, focusing on autobiographical characterisation can show that for all its oddity, the *Wake* treats some of the same concerns as Joyce's earlier works.

Thus in the *Wake*, as in *Exiles*, Joyce's personality appears divided among characters who dramatise its varied and often contradictory potentialities. These characters complement one another more directly than do Stephen and Bloom in *Ulysses*. Stephen and Bloom, presented from essentially different points of view, are beings less complementary than contrasting, as Joyce shows by basing them on his life at points widely separated in time. Shem and Shaun in the *Wake*, like Richard and Robert in *Exiles*, seem to embody simultaneous possibilities. Shem can behave like Shaun and *vice versa*; Robert could have become a Richard, or Richard remained a Robert, but Stephen cannot become Bloom and Bloom was never Stephen. Characters in *Exiles* and the *Wake* seem to interact less naturalistically, more purely subjectively, than do Stephen and Bloom; and they represent continuities within Joyce's character or within his way of perceiving or reporting on his character, rather than the discontinuities embodied in the protagonists of *Ulysses*.

Signs of Joycean characteristics in *Finnegans Wake* are easy to find. It seems that all the characters may at times assume his contours, as if the speculation about author-character links which appeared in the earlier works has led to an earnest desire to explore such links — perhaps to the point of producing a book in which this exploration is possible. Joyce-personae form themselves from apparently fragmentary matter, enact a recognisable deed, attitude or mannerism, then disintegrate, only to recur in altered form. Frequently, a Joyce-persona appears in virtual isolation from its environment, an isolation which seems an extension and parody of Stephen Dedalus' aloofness, and hints at a momentary desire to free the creative self from causal contexts altogether. Little concern with growth appears in the most intensely autobiographical portions of the text, which may bear no obvious relationship to any of the naturalistic or symbolic time-scales of the *Wake*. Joyce now investigates the self as it seeks definition through an attitude or credo or way of life. He probably felt he had analysed his development thoroughly enough in the *Portrait* and *Ulysses* and could now reflect on more static, expansive projections of his personality.

Thus few incidents from Joyce's outer life appear as events in the *Wake*, as his quarrel with Gogarty appeared in *Ulysses*, for example. Allusions to peripheral parts of his life, such as his legal battles and the Henry Carr incident, often seem mere private jokes and no doubt all readers will overlook some allusions of this type.[1] Joyce, indeed, warns of the inadequacy of attempts to understand a person by studying the so-called 'facts' of his life, for 'the unfacts, did we possess them, are too imprecisely few to warrant our certitude' (*FW* 57.16–17). Joyce continues to insist, as he had done in *Ulysses*, on the difficulty of knowing a person's true nature. He seems, indeed, to have become more pessimistic about the possibility.

Joyce, then, seldom appears in action; appropriately enough in a work which is more a retrospective dream than a narrative, more concerned with states than events. His exiled state provides imagery for extended portions of the text, the tone of such references ranging from neutral to melancholy or sardonic. The prevalence of bland references to exile suggests that the inevitability of his state may now be taken for granted: the earlier belligerence has largely disappeared. It is clear that Joyce wishes to be seen as a voluntary exile in control of all possible links to his country and his past. Most of the allusions to people near Joyce involve Nora and Stanislaus, both of whom he persuaded to share his exile. His personal context is to be wholly self-defined.

Certain distinctive Joycean attributes receive consistent attention. Such allusions, often slight in themselves, contribute to Joyce's rather eerie ubiquity in the surface texture of the work. It is as if he wants his book to look like him. References to eyesight, for example, usually involve Joyce's own troublesome eyes: 'a poor acheseyeld from Ailing' (*FW* 148.33) — sore-eyed exile from ailing Ireland — recalls his self-depiction as an 'international eyesore', and 'piteous onewinker' (*FW* 174.19) both invokes his famous eyepatch, mentioned repeatedly in the *Wake* for no apparent reason and links him to Earwicker, through the sound of 'onewinker' and through Earwicker's own tendency to wink. Several passages anatomise moral failings of which Joyce was, with varying degrees of justification, accused — for example, complacent egotism: he 'acts active, peddles in passivism and is a gorgon of selfridgeousness' (*FW* 137.33—34).

Unsurprisingly, many of the specific personal references concern Joyce the writer. Here his tone becomes particularly ironic and whether the irony is gleeful or defensive is not always apparent. The Shem of the seventh chapter embodies every literary failing of which one could accuse Joyce and Shem's kinds of weaknesses provoke attack throughout the *Wake*. He indulges in infelicitous wordplay ('Illstarred punster', *FW* 467.29) and stylistic wilfulness, yet he plagiarises shamelessly. Shaun accuses Shem of stealing his ideas, as Stanislaus, with some justification, had accused Joyce. Shem seizes on the trivial utterances of those around him, being 'covetous of his neighbour's word' (*FW* 172.30), and has no scruples about displaying other people's dirty linen in public. Joyce seems to plead guilty to this last charge by following the 'Shem' chapter with a scene where the washing of other people's dirty linen in public occurs literally. Shem's writing can be childish, sentimental, facile, trivially cathartic, or onanistic. He 'used to stipple endlessly inartistic portraits of himself' (*FW* 182.18—19).

There are hints that Joyce's aim in the *Wake* as in some of his letters may be to appear as a martyr, 'in honour bound to the cross of your own cruelfiction' (*FW* 192.18—19). Joyce mocks the self-conscious artistic integrity he had proclaimed in his early years, remarking of Shem that no writer 'ever nursed such a spoiled opinion of his monstrous marvellosity as did this mental and moral defective' (*FW* 177.15—16). Joyce thus analyses ruthlessly his real, perceived and reported literary failings. Yet by comic and grotesque exaggeration and by presenting real and spurious weaknesses in the same manner Joyce implies that none of his faults should be taken too seriously. He displays his habitual ingenuity in converting vices into virtues, as well as demonstrating, through self-knowledge and the power of expression, his determination to make his own moral and literary decisions.

There is little point in asking whether Shem wrote Joyce's works; partly because Shem is even less separable from his literary context than Stephen is, being perhaps more a linguistic than a psychological creation. Nevertheless, all the works are mentioned in the *Wake*, including *Stephen Hero* if 'sweetheart emmas' (*FW* 328.21) and 'Sh! You are mad!' (*FW* 193.28) recall that novel. References to Joyce's volumes of poetry intensify the condescension already implicit in these volumes' actual titles and allusions to *Dubliners*, like the book itself, seem detached but precise.[2] Some of the allusions to the *Portrait* poke fun at Stephen: 'astundished' (*FW* 187.03); 'wetbed confession' (*FW* 188.01) and 'Up Lancs!' (*FW* 500.11). References to *Ulysses*, the 'usylessly unreadable Blue Book of Eccles' (*FW* 179.26—7) resemble in tone both Shem's self-accusing remarks and Joyce's banter

in letters where he implies that writing *Ulysses* has exhausted
him beyond its merits and he will be glad to see the last of it.

There are parodies of the titles or subjects of the twelve
central episodes of *Ulysses* at *FW* 229.13—16, in phrases
a slightly wittier Leopold Bloom could have devised ('Lestrygonians' becomes 'The Luncher Out' and 'Naughtsycalves'
seem to speak for themselves). A few retrospective interpretations or hints appear: 'Probe loom' (*FW* 286.20) seems
to advise Bloom to watch more closely the weavings of his
Penelope; 'telemac' (*FW* 176.36) teasingly associates M'Intosh
and Stephen-Telemachus, but the 'man in brown about town'
(*FW* 443.20—21) seems to be M'Intosh as Joyce.

The most appealing invocations of Joyce's work, however,
involve the *Wake* itself. Self-parody had been a Joycean habit
before, but never on such a scale. Some of the common
reader's dark suspicions about the book receive darkly sus-
picious confirmation: it is 'a reel of funnish ficts' (*FW*
288.08—09) and 'Funnycoon's Wick' (*FW* 499.13). It parodies
repeatedly its own most delicate or moving moments, such as
the end of the 'Anna Livia' chapter, which seems to have
been one of Joyce's favourite pieces:

— Besides the bubblye waters of babblyebubblye waters of?
— Right (*FW* 526.09—10).

About these overt references to Joyce's life and works
hovers a comic and sometimes spiteful spirit. The allusions
appear almost too simple — which is one reason why we
pounce on them with a sense of relief amid the obscurities
of the *Wake* — and Joyce seems to be testing our assumptions
about their deeper significance. Often, in criticism, the mere
identification of an allusion will be offered as a more
complete explanation of an author's meaning than it really
provides and analyses of the characters of the *Wake* have
been guilty of this tendency to substitute an identity parade
for an investigation of motive. Joyce insists that we think
about the true nature of the ingredients of his book; sometimes by deliberately depriving them of all but surface
meaning and at other times by entangling them in apparently
infinite webs of significance. He thus seems to hint that
surface and depth exist as two facets of the same block, one

reflective and one relatively transparent. One sends us back out of the book, the other (if we can find it) lets us inside.

It should be remembered, then, that the 'surface references' — the kind discussed so far — may run counter to Joyce's central preoccupations, may be, in fact, a calculated disguise, rather like the disguises he assumes in many of his letters. Once we think we have found Joyce, we may feel relieved of the need to search further, however trivial may be those aspects of himself which he has allowed us to see and however false the clues sometimes feel even as we clutch on to them. A complementary critical danger exists here, analogous to over-ingenious allusion-spotting: it is difficult to prove any interpretation of the *Wake* impossible and so one may analyse at any 'depth' with little fear of correction. While Clive Hart's advocacy of conservative readings — assuming only those meanings which are necessary to make sense of a particular passage — is a valid warning, it is a criterion applicable only with reservations to the methods of characterisation used in the book, which may have little apparent connection with the 'necessary' narrative sense of a passage.[3]

Besides, experience of *Ulysses* teaches us that Joyce exploits a multitude of means of communicating which may have little to do with the narrative level of his text. This kind of disconnection between 'what is going on' and 'what is being communicated' is particularly marked in the case of autobiographical character-sketches. The processes which go on in the *Wake* are not directly those of Joyce's life and he appears most frequently in the more static portions of the text, as if he has been waiting for the action to subside before venturing out. Considerable tact must be applied in exploring Joyce's use of his own experience in a work where he has allowed himself innumerable places to hide but made no promise that he will actually be found there.

Joyce hints at the oblique and subtle nature of his self-presentation by directing his narrative attention past his characters into realms inaccessible to them. Much of the *Wake* apparently happens outside the consciousness of the characters; much less of *Ulysses* does and none of the *Portrait* except those ironies we choose to attribute to Joyce rather than to Stephen. In his earlier works, Joyce had allocated some of his creative energy to his protagonists, though he kept these figures at a safe distance by withholding from them parts of his own being (heroism or actual artistic achievement or eloquence, for example): Gabriel Conroy reviews books but does not write them; Stephen seems a less promising writer than Joyce, despite his intelligence and also has a less developed sense of humour; Bloom might like to write but is usually associated rather with the creation of advertisements and is not particularly eloquent. Richard Rowan does produce books, but his personality seems limited and unappealing compared with Joyce's.

No single character in the *Wake* acts in this capacity of reduced but recognisable author substitute. It is an open question whether we can usefully talk of 'single characters' of the kind found in the earlier works in any case, particularly when we are considering Joyce's use of his own experience in depicting them. Joycean energy devolves not only on Shem but on his antagonist Shaun, or divides itself among large groups of characters. The dreamer responsible for the whole book (if we find his presence a useful object of thought) may seem the best analogue for previous authorial personae and his role resembles in one sense that of the older Stephen in the *Portrait* — that is, the person in whose mind the book takes place.

Yet it is doubtful whether the dreamer should be seen as a 'character' within the book. Certainly, Earwicker, to whom the dream is often attributed, cannot dream up the *Wake* any more than Stephen, as we see him, can write *Ulysses*. Any candidates for the role of dreamer would have to resemble Joyce closely. By these means Joyce shows his close involvement with every consciousness in the *Wake* and hence the interrelationship, within his own consciousness, of the qualities they represent or embody. He minimises the distance between work and author, as if seeking to become commensurate with his creation. This desire to erect a structure reproducing Joyce's own vast and complex mental contours hints at a preoccupation with literary self-exploration and revelation of the most insistent kind.

We are thus encouraged to equate work and author in an unprecedented manner. It is fair to read the *Wake* as a final statement about Joyce's consciousness. Though he probably expected to live longer and write more he can hardly, in his late fifties and in severely constricted physical and spiritual circumstances, have contemplated another work on the same scale. So strong is the gravitational power of the book, so striking its ability to assimilate diverse material, that it is difficult to imagine that fragments from its construction could have been easily salvaged for use on a new project (Joyce's usual method of beginning work).

The *Wake* seems in places as preoccupied with its own claim to exist in its actual form as with reference to externally-significant matters. Joyce seeks to emancipate himself from all popular assumptions about how he should write, just as he seeks to evade other people's forms of logic. To the implied assertion that he should write about recognisable people and situations, he responds by taking ordinary personalities and events, then loading them with massive symbolic and archetypal import, as if to show that all people may have such importance. He studiously repudiates facile assumptions about 'naturalistic' characterisation: his characters will behave 'out of character' if he chooses, behave with the arbitrariness and inconsistency shown by real people, respond to events with exaggerated fear or guilt or with evasions of logic.

By repeated self-contradiction, especially in the presentation of Shem, Joyce probes radically our belief in the continuity of a literary or actual personality, so reinforcing in an additional way his strategy of distributing his own personality into apparently inhospitable portions of his work. Similarly, if he is told to use his words to denote objects and concepts familiar to others, he replies by demonstrating his need to use language in ever more elaborate ways and to establish it as the legitimate object of his own most concentrated attention, pushing the relationship of word and object into new degrees of unanimity. Joyce expressed irritation at attempts to summarise works of literature, insisting that their nature was thereby destroyed: they exist only as a function of the language which constitutes them, not by virtue of what they may happen to depict. Reality resides in form more than in content; or, rather, content can only exist as a function of form (Joyce seems weakest where this relationship threatens to break down in his own work, as it occasionally does in *Stephen Hero* or *Exiles*).

The *Wake*, for all its idiosyncrasy, accords with this aesthetic assumption at least. If it were suggested that Joyce should establish some means of making value-judgments of his characters, he would no doubt reply that he seeks to give his analysis all the complexity of the self he analyses, especially when it is his own self. He had always shown through his distinctive manner of complicating his works that his life must be seen as correspondingly irreducible, and *Finnegans Wake* merely makes that assertion more explicitly and emphatically than he had made it before. The book is designed to provide no solutions more final than life provides and it may be no more comprehensible: Joyce did say that it would take a lifetime to understand it. He wanted to define himself by proving his ability constantly to find and orchestrate new forms, as if in compensation for the imagination he claimed to lack. In the *Wake* he has ensured that his secrets will be yielded only gradually, that the work will embody the continuity of its own creative processes and hence of his struggles to shape it in a way no other literary work had ever attempted to achieve.

Yet even if we accept and understand this deep identification of author and text, considerable problems remain. The *Wake* illustrates the difficulty of communicating an impression of the whole being which can satisfy the writer without mystifying the reader. It shows that characters so difficult for readers to relate to their own experience can attract only limited sympathy, readers being as egotistical as authors. Moreover, Joyce seems at times so preoccupied with the means of observing that observation itself lapses, as though the narrative stance of 'Ithaca' and style of 'Oxen of the Sun' were superimposed on the slight subject-matter of one of his poems. It is possible to over-refine a stance to the point where little can be seen from it. The *Wake* sometimes seems so self-absorbed that the objects of its knowledge are lost. Possible perspectives multiply until the canvas blurs; double visions sustain themselves perilously for a moment, then dissolve.

In the *Wake* Joyce seems to seek an all-encompassing point of view. But such a view readily becomes diffuse. Joyce may have known what he was doing at each moment and what each linguistic fragment signified, but he may have placed too much faith in the ability of readers to reconstruct his intentions. The *Wake* is full of fast-moving glimpses which are frequently striking in themselves but also perplexing in the kinds of relationship with context they suppose. Point of view seems to give way to the voracious appetite of the text itself: as the puns and allusions multiply, a controlling point of view becomes increasingly difficult to sustain. No doubt Joyce undercuts assumptions about point of view deliberately, as he does those about character and something of the same kind happens in the later sections of *Ulysses* as well. Yet it is doubtful whether the result in the *Wake* is the production of a more flexible sensitivity to meaning, as Joyce apparently intends. More often, the protean viewpoint makes it difficult to discern anything but the shapes with any confidence. Joyce's mode may enact the texture of a dream, but he intends more than the creation of an impression of dreaming. Meanings inhabit the text but their capture, by anyone except Joyce, remains problematic. A reader's desire for more attainable viewpoints may be no more naïve than Joyce's assumption that we can do without them.

Thus the 'surface' of *Finnegans Wake* is relatively easy to detach for scrutiny, but the book's deeper being, however refreshing Joyce's iconoclasm, energy and ingenuity cause it to be, constantly upsets attempts to come to terms with it. No single aspect like characterisation can be isolated for discussion without some consideration, however brief or implicit, of everything else in the book; everything is defined by contexts, yet those contexts are just as elusive and changeable as what they supposedly define. The self-preoccupation of the *Wake* equals and discloses Joyce's own. Its introspection, its constant assertions of recurrence, reflect his own attitudes, preoccupations or wishes. The work enacts the fusions and transfusions of memory, both encouraging and discouraging the reader's power to remember what he has read.

If Joyce seems to tease and frustrate his readers more than he intended, it may be useful to investigate what the *Wake* is doing for him and how the characters bear meaning when seen from his point of view. The *Wake* is Joyce's most assertively 'confessional' work, as though his difficult language and the elusive people that language creates act as masks behind which he can bare his soul in a way which is not possible in the relatively circumstantial *Portrait* and *Ulysses*.

The dominant moral concern of the *Wake* is with guilt and attempts to deal with guilt. Such concerns animate much of the *Portrait, Exiles* and *Ulysses* as well, but in those cases Joyce circumscribes the guilt by specifying its causes and attributing it to particular characters. Earwicker's unspecified sin in the park seems to release a disproportionate amount of guilt not only because it echoes the Fall but because its nature cannot be precisely determined. Attempts to evade guilt by trying to hide or confuse its causes thus form one of the book's central preoccupations. It is, inevitably, tempting to speculate about biographical bases for such concerns and Joyce's anxiety about his effects on his children's lives comes to mind, as his anxiety about his effects on Nora's life does in the case of *Exiles*, though in its most intense form (worry about Lucia's increasing mental disorders) such anxiety could have influenced only later-written portions of the text. It is Lucia who 'tears up lettereens she never apposed a pen upon' (*FW* 276.06-07). Such psychological speculations cannot properly be pursued here, though they are plausible enough.[4]

Whatever his extra-literary motives may have been, in any case, Joyce's determination to explore the emotions of self-doubt and remorse on a massive scale seems indisputable. His characters are accused of a vast array of failings, ranging from Shem's plagiarism to Earwicker's mysterious, though earth-shaking, sin in the park. The circumstances producing guilt may be exaggerated to emphasise the extent of the guilt Joyce actually felt, as with Stephen's remorse about his mother's death in *Ulysses*, but it seems that in the *Wake* the exaggeration goes beyond the requirements of that particular strategy. Yet the characters also appear in and define themselves through their attempts to overcome their guilt, which often take the form of nervous jests. Life, for Joyce in his later years, increasingly becomes a painful business made tolerable by laughter ('Loud, heap miseries upon us yet entwine our arts with laughters low', *FW* 259.07-08). The coexistence of the real pain of remorse with the necessary transcendence of it, by humorous understanding of its place or lack of place in the scheme of things, marks much of Joyce's work from Stephen's earliest musings to the end of the *Wake*. In his last book he takes on all sins, but by making art from them he becomes a martyr on his own terms. He appreciates that guilt is basic to his behaviour, as to human behaviour generally and labours to come to terms with it.

Thus the *Wake* includes a cathartic function among its many identities. Yet it also accepts. Its multiple, complex, unstable and intermingling characters establish a sense of perilous, strident but vital community. Joyce acknowledges, in however idiosyncratic a manner, the resemblance between his life and other lives. Having defined himself initially by stressing his difference from others, as the *Portrait* shows, Joyce approaches in the *Wake* a definition based on resemblances, admitting close analogies and bonds with those around him. His manner of writing remains perplexing, but it does not show that he has isolated himself from humanity; rather, he wants to incorporate as much as possible of what other people have made of the world. In his own terms (and Joyce did nothing except in his own terms) he has never been more human. He seems to acknowledge in the *Wake* that the most 'private' areas of the soul may be, paradoxically, the aspects we can most readily share, because despite our linguistic and other differences from one another, we all use similar means to conceal those areas.

For all its difficulty and even perversity, then, the *Wake* should also be seen as a gesture of reconciliation. Joyce pours both self and world into his book, exploiting every possible interaction between. He admits the continuity between his life and other lives, domesticating and validating the theme of cyclic recurrence, for all the strangeness of the text in which this process occurs. Yet he still insists on the right to investigate his material from his own peculiar angles, maintaining to the last that independence of vision which he had proclaimed in his earliest work.

7

Conclusion

Studies of characterisation are intrinsically interesting and could be defended on the grounds that they inform us about the ways in which authors work even where they do not seem necessary to the interpretation of a text. Often, however, studies of the source and treatment of characters will directly inform reading, either by uncovering apposite facts whose disclosure an author may not have anticipated or, more importantly, by unearthing information which the author has for some reason concealed with the intention that it should eventually be found. In the case of Joyce, meaning often resides in the nature of his sources and his manner of treating them and he often hides information for readers to discover in due course.

Joyce must have known that future scholars would pry into his life in quest of material to help explain his works. (There is a list of addresses in *Finnegans Wake* which makes little sense unless we know that these were Joyce's own addresses.) Nobody seems to have asked what Joyce thought the results of such investigations would be and perhaps it is pointless to speculate. But it does seem certain that he created his characters in the knowledge that newly-discovered facts about his life would be brought to bear on their interpretation. Such information, like knowledge of the factual details of historical Dublin, therefore becomes a legitimate aid to analysis.

For Joyce, meaning is also conveyed through the variety of modes of characterisation among his major works. The progression from *Dubliners* to *Finnegans Wake* can be measured by noting what kinds of characters appear and what happens to them, as well as by attention to the more conspicuously radical changes in literary technique from book to book. In *Dubliners*, examples of autobiographical characterisation exist, but they are mostly oblique and ironic, used to contrast the detached artist figure with a prevailing benighted environment; while in *Stephen Hero*, written at the same time, there is an anxious preoccupation with the status of the autobiographical figure which is appealing but by Joyce's later standards undisciplined and unsteady. The *Portrait* copes with this problem by a rigorous formal organisation and by elevating the process of the quest for origins and for self-understanding into a central theme in its own right (as well as an exploration necessary to Joyce's subsequent works).

Exiles investigates 'dramatic' elements of character-conflict, drawing on Joyce's own personality and circumstances for basic material. The length and complexity of *Ulysses* permit a fuller treatment of the interplay between 'the self' and 'the other', a theme anticipated in *Exiles*, as well as a consideration of the relationship between 'the self' and 'the world', a theme adumbrated but not directly confronted in the *Portrait*. The sensitivity and attention to detail which *Ulysses* manifests also emphasise the uniqueness of each person and the need to acknowledge this uniqueness in any attempt to overcome solipsism. The intricacy and urbanity of the novel's modes of characterisation help to convey this implication. Stephen, a character whose shape Joyce said could not be changed, is joined by Bloom, whose ability to change his psychological shape and adapt to different surroundings appears as part of his strength and part of the lesson he could teach Stephen. Joyce's juxtaposition of these two characters shows his new personal allegiance to such values as Bloom embodies.

In *Finnegans Wake* Joyce goes further, to stress what we all have in common; people in this book are variable and seem to melt into each other, so that emphasis falls on shared characteristics rather than the unique characters dominant in Joyce's earlier works. Here Joyce fully acknowledges his own participation in the flux of personality and the flux of history. As Ellmann puts it, 'in *A Portrait of the Artist as a Young Man* Joyce had demonstrated the repetition of traits in the first twenty years of one person's life; in *Ulysses* he had displayed this repetition in the day of two persons; in *Finnegans Wake* he displayed it in the lives of everyone' (*JJ* 716).

These developments and relationships are all given substance by Joyce's modes of characterisation, which thus bear a vital share of the load of meaning in each case. But there are other reasons for Joyce's emphasis on characterisation which also need to be remembered.

Characterisation is particularly vital in Joyce because almost nothing exists in his work except in relation to a character's mind. Joyce's dislike of exposition and omniscient description, itself an attitude which needs further investigation, leads him to make his characters into containers of narrative energy as well as subjects of the narrative, even in an early story such as 'Eveline'. He tries as far as possible to have his characters depict themselves, rather than employing a narrator to perform this task. Information is conveyed not by a detached narrator but by a narrator or narrative voice able to imitate, enhance or limit the sensibility of a particular character. Joyce's works thus exist as a balance of forces which are energised and organised by the magnetic power of the characters he depicts.

Moreover, one of Joyce's most central aesthetic principles — that style should express subject as fully as possible, that form and content should be inseparable — is intimately related to his modes of characterisation. This principle of fusion between substance and statement commits him to a kind of literary ventriloquism which ensures that the characters' voices (and hence, presumably, personalities) will colour every corner of the text.

Finally, the strength and solidity of Joyce's characterisation is closely related to his use of real models, just as the seriousness of his treatment of subjective experience is validated by his use of himself as a model. This method gives to his characters the same kind of realism attained in his works by the use of actual locations in Dublin. Joyce's characters, indeed, become more realistic than his settings. They do so partly because other novelists also use real settings but few use real personalities as assiduously as Joyce does; in terms of our comparative expectations, then, the realism of his characters is particularly striking. The characters also predominate over the settings because Joyce pays them far more attention. Even in *Ulysses*, the environment is never as fully realised as Joyce implied when he said that Dublin, if destroyed, could be rebuilt by the use of his books as a blueprint. With rare exceptions, as in parts of 'Wandering Rocks', we see only what the characters see of the city. Joyce's works are all delicately poised between actuality and fiction, with great ingenuity employed in reshaping the real world into a fictional world, but also with great care taken to ensure that actuality remains present not only in a concealed or metaphorical form but in the shape of craggy outcrops.

Joyce's concern with this relationship between reality and fiction further substantiates detailed analysis of the ways in which he constructs his characters. Joyce's modes of characterisation and of self-portraiture show not only the desire to create a certain type of character, but also his allegiance to a certain attitude to reality. This attitude remains essentially one of respect and affection, which the difficulty and occasional perversity of his writing never completely conceal. Joyce may have based his characters so firmly on directly observed reality because of the supposed lack of imagination which he himself lamented. But there is a more profound and more positive reason for this adherence to actuality. Joyce also wanted to show that the world he envisaged in his books was, in fact, the real world.

Notes

Chapter 1
INTRODUCTION
(pp. 1–12)

1 In Hart and Hayman, *James Joyce's Ulysses*, 57.
2 C. C. Walcutt, *Man's Changing Mask*, 302.
3 Seymour Chatman, *Story and Discourse*, 113.
4 W. J. Harvey, *Character and the Novel*, 32.
5 'Setting' could include people who never achieve the status of characters: a 'busy street scene' would in most cases implicitly contain pedestrians, but we might never meet them as individuals.
6 See Chatman, 125.
7 Philip Stevick, *The Theory of the Novel*, 222.
8 Jonathan Culler surveys some of these attempts in *Structuralist Poetics*, 230–38. Culler acknowledges that 'character is the major aspect of the novel to which structuralism has paid least attention and has been least successful in treating' (230).
9 Harvey, 184.
10 Vladimir Nabokov, *Lectures on Literature*, 286. Later in this lecture on *Ulysses* Nabokov apparently relents, slightly, commenting that Stephen and Bloom are both 'wanderers and exiles, and . . . in both runs the singing blood of James Joyce, their maker' (355).
11 Hart and Hayman, 342.

Chapter 2
DUBLINERS
(pp. 13–29)

1 A surprising claim, since Ellmann believes that James Flynn in 'The Sisters', for example, was based on a priest related to Joyce's mother. See *MBK* 62; *JJ* 20, 163.
2 Stanislaus Joyce points out some of these; see *MBK* 41.
3 See *Dubliners: A Facsimile of Drafts and Manuscripts* (*James Joyce Archive*), 129.
4 Joyce implied that this image in the *Portrait* betokens the transition from one stage of life to the next; see *L II* 79.
5 See, for example, Sondra Melzer, 'In the Beginning there was "Eveline"', *JJQ*, 16 (1979), 479–85.

6 This connection has been pointed out before though much of the evidence which supports it has not. See, for example, Albert J. Solomon, 'The Backgrounds of "Eveline"', *Eire-Ireland*, 6, 3 (Fall 1971), 23—38.

7 See Eric Partridge, *A Dictionary of Slang and Unconventional English*, Vol. I, 101. Another possible connotation of Buenos Aires for Joyce involved the model for Dante Riordan, Mrs Hearn Conway, whose husband fled to Buenos Aires with her money. Such connotations, though not active in the story, might support those critics who argue that Frank is a deceiver who has no intention of marrying Eveline.

8 The best available reproduction of this photograph appears in *L II*, opposite the first page of text.

Chapter 3
A PORTRAIT OF THE ARTIST AS A YOUNG MAN
(pp. 30—48)

1 Kenner, *Joyce's Voices*, 21.

2 Gogarty's removal from the *Portrait* may have occurred because Joyce came to envisage a role for him in *Ulysses* which would be better served if he appeared there for the first time.

3 Kevin Sullivan, *Joyce among the Jesuits*, 164.

4 The relationship between this ugliness and Stephen's aesthetic has also been discussed by Richard Peterson, 'Stephen's Aesthetics: Reflections of the Artist or the Ass?', *JJQ*, 17 (1980), 427—33.

5 See Edmund Epstein, *The Ordeal of Stephen Dedalus*, 115—16.

6 While on the subject of Joyce's and Stephen's relations with their parents, we might observe that at the beginning of the *Portrait* Stephen's father 'always gave him a shilling when he asked for sixpence' (*P* 26), while at the end of the novel Stephen says that he 'asked [his mother] for sixpence. Got threepence' (*P* 248). These transactions may reflect wryly on the changing family fortunes but perhaps also suggest that Stephen feels he gets more than he needs or deserves from his father, less from his mother.

7 Frank Budgen, *James Joyce and the Making of Ulysses*, 52.

Chapter 4
EXILES
(pp. 49—65)

1 See *JJ* 78—80 for an account of Joyce's early play.

2 In the manuscript versions of 'A Painful Case', Joyce mentions a 'Dr Cosgrave, assistant house surgeon of Vincent's hospital' (*Dubliners: A Facsimile of Drafts and Manuscripts*, 119, 165). This name, which looks like an allusion to Joyce's friend, was removed about 1909, perhaps because Joyce no longer felt inclined to joke about him.

3 Sheldon Brivic, 'Structure and Meaning in Joyce's *Exiles*', *JJQ*, 6 (1968), 29—52.

Chapter 5
ULYSSES
(pp. 66–103)
1 Comments from people who have read *Ulysses* but not the *Portrait* seem to support the view that Stephen is less appealing in *Ulysses* if his *Portrait* background is unknown.
2 See Hans Walter Gabler, 'Stephen in Paris', *JJQ*, 17 (1980), 306–11.
3 See *JJ* 143–79.
4 Kenner, *Ulysses*, 55.
5 R. P. Blackmur, 'The Jew in Search of a Son: Joyce's *Ulysses*', in *Eleven Essays in the European Novel*, 43.
6 Adams, *Surface and Symbol*, 106.
7 See *JJ* 418–19.
8 See *L II* 47n.
9 For an appraisal of negative and other interpretations of the novel's ending, see Richard M. Kain, 'The Significance of Stephen's Meeting Bloom: A Survey of Interpretations', *JJQ*, 10 (1972), 147–60.

Chapter 6
FINNEGANS WAKE
(pp. 104–117)
1 See *JJ* 439–72.
2 See 'shamebred music' (*FW* 164.15–16); 'chambermade music' (*FW* 184.04); 'Eche bennyache' (*FW* 302.28). The titles of all the *Dubliners* stories appear on *FW* 186–7.
3 See Clive Hart, *Structure and Motif in Finnegans Wake*, 29–31.
4 Ellmann avoids mentioning this connection specifically when he discusses the *Wake* but notes 'the possibility that a more regular family life might have prevented her illness invaded and occupied Joyce's mind. He did not disavow guilt; he embraced it eagerly . . . He identified himself closely with her.' Again, 'Joyce had had difficulty . . . in working out the final aspects of *Finnegans Wake*, and saw Lucia's turmoil during the same period as parallel to his own.' See *JJ* 650, 662.

Bibliography

Adams, R. M. *Surface and Symbol: The Consistency of James Joyce's Ulysses*, New York: Oxford Univ. Press 1962.

Benstock, Shari, and Bernard Benstock, *Who's He when He's at Home: A James Joyce Directory*, Urbana: Univ. of Illinois Press, 1980.

Bidwell, Bruce, and Linda Heffer, *The Joycean Way: A Topographic Guide to Dubliners and A Portrait of the Artist as a Young Man*, Dublin: Wolfhound Press, 1981.

Blackmur, R. P. 'The Jew in Search of a Son: Joyce's *Ulysses*'. In *Eleven Essays in the European Novel*, New York: Harcourt, Brace & World, 1964, 27—47.

Brivic, Sheldon. 'Structure and Meaning in Joyce's *Exiles*', *JJQ*, 6 (1968), 29—52.

Budgen, Frank, *James Joyce and the Making of Ulysses, and Other Writings*, London: Oxford Univ. Press, 1972.

Chatman, Seymour, *Story and Discourse: Narrative Structure in Fiction and Film*, Ithaca: Cornell Univ. Press, 1978.

Culler, Jonathan, *Structuralist Poetics: Structuralism, Linguistics and the Study of Literature*, London: Routledge & Kegan Paul, 1975.

Ellmann, Richard, *Ulysses on the Liffey*, London, Faber & Faber, 1972.

Epstein, Edmund, *The Ordeal of Stephen Dedalus: The Conflict of the Generations in James Joyce's A Portrait of the Artist as a Young Man*, Carbondale: Southern Illinois Univ. Press, 1971.

Gabler, Hans Walter, 'Stephen in Paris', *JJQ*, 17 (1980), 306—11.

Glasheen, Adaline, *Third Census of Finnegans Wake: An Index of the Characters and their Roles*, Berkeley: Univ. of California Press, 1977.

Gordon, John, *James Joyce's Metamorphoses*, Dublin: Gill & Macmillan, 1981.

Groden, Michael, *Ulysses in Progress*, Princeton: Princeton Univ. Press, 1977.

Groden, Michael, and Hans Walter Gabler, David Hayman, A. Walton Litz, and Danis Rose, edd. *The James Joyce Archive*, New York: Garland, 1978—9.

Hart, Clive, *Structure and Motif in Finnegans Wake*, London: Faber & Faber, 1962.

Hart, Clive, and David Hayman, edd. *James Joyce's Ulysses: Critical Essays*, Berkeley: Univ. of California Press, 1974.

Harvey, W. J. *Character and the Novel*, London: Chatto & Windus, 1965.

Kain, Richard M. 'The Significance of Stephen's Meeting Bloom: A Survey of Interpretations', *JJQ*, 10 (1972), 147–60.

Kenner, Hugh, *Dublin's Joyce*, London: Chatto & Windus, 1955.

Kenner, Hugh, *Joyce's Voices*, Berkeley: Univ. of California Press, 1978.

Kenner, Hugh, *Ulysses*, London: George Allen & Unwin, 1980.

Lawrence, Karen, *The Odyssey of Style in Ulysses*, Princeton: Princeton Univ. Press, 1981.

MacNicholas, John, *James Joyce's Exiles: A Textual Companion*, New York: Garland, 1979.

Maddox, James H., *Joyce's Ulysses and the Assault upon Character*, New Brunswick, N. J.: Rutgers Univ. Press, 1978.

Melzer, Sondra, 'In the Beginning there was "Eveline"', *JJQ*, 16 (1979), 479–85.

Nabokov, Vladimir, *Lectures on Literature*, ed. Fredson Bowers, New York: Harcourt Brace Jovanovich, 1980.

Partridge, Eric, *A Dictionary of Slang and Unconventional English*, London: Routledge & Kegan Paul, 1961.

Peake, C. H., *James Joyce: The Citizen and the Artist*, London: Edward Arnold, 1977.

Peterson, Richard, 'Stephen's Aesthetics: Reflections of the Artist or the Ass?', *JJQ*, 17 (1980), 427–33.

Raleigh, J. H., *The Chronicle of Leopold and Molly Bloom: Ulysses as Narrative*, Berkeley: Univ. of California Press, 1977.

Scholes, Robert, and Richard M. Kain, edd. *The Workshop of Daedalus: James Joyce and the Raw Materials for A Portrait of the Artist as a Young Man*, Evanston: Northwestern Univ. Press, 1965.

Solomon, Albert J., 'The Backgrounds of "Eveline"', *Eire-Ireland*, 6, 3 (Fall 1971), 23–38.

Steinberg, Erwin R., *The Stream of Consciousness and Beyond in Ulysses*, Pittsburg: Univ. of Pittsburgh Press, 1973.

Stevick, Philip, ed. *The Theory of the Novel*, New York: Free Press, 1967.

Sullivan, Kevin, *Joyce among the Jesuits*, New York: Columbia Univ. Press, 1958.

Walcutt, C. C. *Man's Changing Mask: Modes and Methods of Characterization in Fiction*, Minneapolis: Univ. of Minnesota Press, 1966.

Index